I0459007

MASTER YOUR MIND And AVOID BURNOUTS

What Does The Bible Have To Say About This?

Harrison S Mungal, PhD., PsyD.

MASTER YOUR MIND AND AVOID BURNOUTS

Copyright © 2025 Harrison S. Mungal

Unless otherwise identified, Scripture quotations are from New King James Version of the Bible.

Contact author via email:
hsmungal@hotmail.com
info@agetoage.ca
www.agetoage.ca
www.harrisonmungal.com
Facebook: Harrison Mungal
Twitter: AgeToAgeInc1
LinkedIn: Harrison Mungal, Ph.D., PsyD
YouTube: Harrison Mungal
Phone: 905-533-1334

ABOUT *the*

AUTHOR

Harrison Mungal, PhD, PsyD

Dr. Mungal has two doctoral degrees, one in Clinical Psychology and the other in Philosophy in Social Work, dual master's degrees in Social Work and Christian Counselling, and a Bachelor degree in Theology. He worked over 20 years in the fields of mental health and psychiatry then went into psychology. He worked with people from a wide range of backgrounds, including brain injury survivors, refugees, victims of war, PTSD victims, those struggling with mental health and in crisis. He liaison with police, hospitals, community agencies, and inpatient mental health settings.

Dr. Mungal is completely dedicated to improving the lives of his clients. He is known all over the world in over 47 nations for his deep knowledge of neuroscience, mental health, biblical studies and topics supporting individuals, couples and families and businesses.

Dr. Mungal is a highly sought-after workshop presenter who uses his practical approach to help understand the functionality of psychology and spirituality. His global impact is clear from the way he uses humour and enthusiasm to make complicated talks about mental health, addiction, relationships, and parenting at conferences, seminars, and media platforms.

Dr. Mungal's new and scientifically sound methods have been

praised by many institutions, earning him awards and recogniztions. He spreads his influence by training and advising a wide range of community partners, such as respected professionals in the fields of medicine, social work, first responders, law enforcement, and senior management teams.

Dr. Mungal is a leader in cutting-edge cognitive research that looks at mental health issues like addiction, psychosis, anxiety, and depression. His work includes research on music therapy and schizophrenia, substance abuse and addictions in the food service industry, and vaccination for children under six years old.

Dr. Mungal practical therapeutic toolbox includes evidence-based therapies including Cognitive Behavioural Therapy (CBT), Cognitive Processing Therapy (CPT), Dialectical Behavioural Therapy (DBT), Thought Developmental Practice (TDP), Acceptance and Commitment Therapy (ACT). Interpersonal therapy (IPT), Motivational Interviewing Techniques, Grounding Techniques, Integrative Eclectic Therapy, Humanistic Experiential Therapy, Interpersonal Therapy, Supportive Therapy, Exposure Therapy, Visual Therapy, Psychodynamic Therapy.

TABLE OF CONTENTS

INTRODUCTION...7

MASTERING THE MIND...15

RESTRUCTURING THE MIND......................................23

TRAINING THE MIND..31

FEEDING THE MIND...39

COACHING THE MIND..47

DECLUTTERING THE MIND..51

WEEDING THE MIND..59

RECONDITIONING THE MIND....................................67

REGROUPING THE MIND..75

MAINTAINING THE MIND...87

RENEWING THE MIND 95

BRAIN DUMPING.. 101

MIND BURNOUT... 111

THINK TANDEM.. 119

AN AFFECTED MIND.. 125

A BURNOUT MIND... 143

A HURT MIND 157

A CONGESTED MIND... 165

A COMBUSTED MIND.. 171

A NOISY MIND... 183

A RESILIENCE MIND 189

CONCLUSION.. 195

INTRODUCTION

You are holding in your hands something far more valuable than another self-help book. This is a rescue manual for the most important three pounds of tissue you will ever own: your brain.

Your mind is the control tower of your entire existence. Every emotion you feel, every decision you make, every relationship you build or break, every dream you chase or abandon, every act of worship or rebellion, every moment of peace or panic originates in that small space between your ears. When the control tower is functioning beautifully, life feels like a symphony. When it is congested, wounded, noisy, or burning, life becomes a screaming fire alarm with no off switch.

Most of us today are walking around with minds that are quietly on fire. We call it "stress," "overwhelm," or "just a season," but the truth is far more serious: millions of us are living in chronic mental burnout without even knowing the clinical name for what is happening inside our skulls.

We keep pushing, scrolling, hustling, comparing, performing, perfecting, and numbing until one day we simply cannot push anymore. The crash is rarely dramatic; it is usually quiet. A tear that won't stop. A panic attack in the grocery store. A sudden inability to get out of bed. A rage that explodes at the people we love most. Or the slow, deadening realization that we no longer feel anything at all.

That is burnout. And it is not a personality flaw. It is not a lack of discipline. It is not a sign that you are weak or lazy or "just not cut out for this." Burnout is the predictable result of running a high-performance machine on empty, contaminated fuel while never changing the oil, rotating the tires, or allowing it to rest.

The staggeringly hope-filled news is this: God did not design your brain to end in flames. He designed it to be renewed, restored, and mastered. Romans 12:2 is not a suggestion; it is a divine promise and a physiological fact: ***"Do not conform to the pattern of this world, but be transformed by the renewing of your mind."***

The same God who spoke galaxies into existence wired your brain with breathtaking neuroplasticity, the proven ability to rewire, heal, and upgrade itself when given the right conditions.

This book is the field guide to creating those conditions. We are going to walk together through every stage of the journey, from the moment you first realize something is wrong to the day you look back and say with a grin, "*I didn't just survive; I became unstoppable.*"

We begin where every honest journey must begin: recognition. We will gently but unflinchingly help you see how your mind has been affected, shaped, coloured, and often distorted by life's relentless input. Words spoken over you as a child. Wounds you never asked for. Comparisons you never meant to make. Cultural noise you never chose to let in. "***For as he thinks in his heart, so is he***" (Proverbs 23:7 NKJV). Until you identify what has affected your mind, you will keep allowing yesterday's voices to write tomorrow's story.

From there we move to understanding the true nature of a burnout mind. Burnout is not laziness wearing a suit; it is emotional, mental, and spiritual exhaustion caused by prolonged, unrelenting stress. You will discover the seven hidden stages most people never see coming, the difference between normal tiredness and dangerous depletion, and the physiological reality that chronic stress actually shrinks the decision-making and memory centers of your brain. More importantly, you will be given the early-warning system God built into your body and spirit so you never have to crash again.

Some pain is loud. Some pain is quiet. Both leave scars on the mind. Betrayal, abuse, abandonment, failure, grief; these are not just "events" that happened; they are neurological injuries.

We will walk through the science of how trauma rewires the brain for hyper-vigilance and how the Holy Spirit partners with modern neuroscience to bring genuine healing. "***He heals the brokenhearted and binds up their wounds***" (Psalm 147:3) is not poetry; it is brain surgery performed by the Great Physician.

Then we confront the congestion, the noise, and the terrifying moment when the mind literally combusts: panic attacks, rage episodes, emotional shutdowns, physical collapse.

You will learn why the average person today receives more information in one week than people a century ago received in a lifetime, and you will be given practical, biblical tools to turn down the volume before the fire starts.

The healing begins in earnest with the simplest, most powerful habit most people have never tried: brain dumping. Ten minutes with a pen and paper can drain an ocean of mental chaos and give you back clarity you thought was gone forever.

We will walk you step-by-step through multiple forms (timed free-writing, mind-mapping, sticky-note storms, prayer journaling) and show you why King David, Habakkuk, and the apostle Paul were master brain-dumpers long before the term existed.

Once the floodwaters are drained, it's time for brain weeding. Just as a garden cannot thrive when choked by weeds, neither can a mind. You will learn how to identify recurring toxic thoughts (insecurity, bitterness, envy, fear of man, perfectionism, shame) and how to uproot them at the root using Scripture, cognitive tools, and Spirit-led repentance. *"Whatever is true... think about such things"* (Philippians 4:8) is not positive thinking; it is aggressive spiritual gardening.

With the weeds gone, we turn to brain decluttering. Decluttering is not just for closets. A cluttered physical environment creates a cluttered mind, and a cluttered digital life guarantees a cluttered soul. You will receive a complete playbook for decluttering your home, your schedule, your devices, and your commitments so your brain has literal space to breathe.

Survival is not the goal; thriving is. We move beyond burnout into a life that is burnout-resistant by design. Sabbath rhythms, soul-care disciplines, boundary-setting as an act of worship, and the lost art of delight become your new normal.

Your brain is not fixed; it is flexible. Neuroplasticity is God's gift that keeps on giving. You will discover how to use Scripture meditation, gratitude practice, worship, confession, fasting, and cognitive-behavioural techniques to literally regrow and strengthen the parts of your brain that stress has damaged. We explore brain reconditioning, restructuring, and regrouping until your mind no longer reacts the way it used to; it responds the way Jesus would.

Jesus-followers train their minds the way elite athletes train their bodies. You will receive daily mental workouts that build focus, emotional regulation, resilience, and spiritual sensitivity. From breath prayer to memory verses to deliberate gratitude to silence and solitude, these are the drills that turn good brains into great ones.

You will learn what to feed your brain and what to starve. Garbage in, garbage out is not a cliché; it is neurology. We give you a biblical and practical guide to curating a diet of truth, beauty, and goodness that literally nourishes your brain cells and starves anxiety.

Just as a high-performance car needs regular maintenance, so does a high-performance mind. You will build a personal maintenance plan that includes sleep, movement, nutrition, community, therapy when needed, and above all, daily encounter with the living God who *"renews your youth like the eagle's"* (Psalm 103:5).

Resilience is not the absence of pressure; it is the presence of Jesus in the pressure. You will learn the science and Scripture behind bounce-back ability and how to cultivate the spiritual muscle that says, *"I can do all things through Christ who strengthens me"* (Philippians 4:13) and actually means it.

You were never meant to think alone. You will discover the beautiful mystery of thinking in tandem with the Holy Spirit, having your thoughts aligned with, corrected by, and empowered by the Mind of Christ (1 Corinthians 2:16).

And we finish exactly where Scripture finishes: brain renewal and brain mastering. This is where *"renewing your mind"* stops being a verse on a coffee mug and becomes your daily, moment-by-moment reality.

You will learn how to take every thought captive, how to master impulsivity, how to live from a place of peace that truly does surpass understanding, and how to walk in the freedom and authority Christ died to give you.

Friend, if you are tired of living with a mind that feels like a war zone, this book is your ceasefire agreement. If you are desperate for peace but terrified that "quiet" might never be possible again, this book is your proof that it is. If you have been told that anxiety, depression, burnout, or racing thoughts are "just who you are," this book is your declaration of war on that lie.

You were not created to merely cope. You were created to rule and reign in life through Christ Jesus (Romans 5:17). And the first territory He wants you to govern is the one between your ears.

I have walked through the fire myself. I know what it is to wake up at 2 a.m. with a heart racing so fast I was certain I was dying. I know the shame of crying in a parked car because the noise in my head was unbearable. And I know the indescribable freedom of discovering that Jesus is not only willing but eager to renew, rewire, and restore every exhausted neuron.

He did it for me. He is doing it now for tens of thousands who have applied these principles. And He is waiting to do it for you.

The world will keep shouting. The demands will keep coming. The notifications will never stop. But you, child of God, do not have to keep burning.

Turn the page. Take a deep breath. The healing has already begun.

Welcome to the journey of mastering your mind and stepping into the peace, power, and purpose you were born for.

You are not broken beyond repair. You are fearfully and wonderfully made.

And your mind is about to become the most powerful weapon of love and light the enemy has ever seen.

MASTERING
THE MIND

MASTERING

the MIND

The mind is the most powerful gift we were created with, along with the heart, and if we do not use our minds correctly, it can be highly destructive. "***For as he thinks in his heart, so is he***" (Proverbs 23:7 NKJV).

The thoughts flowing through our minds can be a blessing or a curse. The thoughts we entertain affect our perception and how we interpret information. We all struggle from time to time with our complex thinking patterns. However, with the help of divergent thinking and, above all, the truth of God's Word, we can set our minds free: "***It is for freedom that Christ has set us free***" (Galatians 5:1).

We need to let our thoughts flow smoothly but should not allow them to rule us. Our thoughts can run wildly if we do not take control of them: "***We demolish arguments and every pretension that sets itself*** *up against the knowledge of God, and we take captive every thought to make it obedient to Christ*" (2 Corinthians 10:5, NIV).

Controlling our thoughts is like raising children. If we do not master parenting, our children will walk all over us. They will then bring shame and disrespect upon themselves and their families. Similarly, lacking control over the mind will bring negative consequences.

Unwanted thoughts that reside in our minds will create unproductive and unhealthy thinking. Changing our thinking to dispel such thoughts will eventually allow us to control our behaviours. This scripture I have been focusing on this book is *"Do not conform to the pattern of this world, but be transformed by the renewing of your mind*" (Romans 12:2).

Mastering the mind involves managing the thoughts that flow through the mind. It involves reprogramming our thinking. This takes skill, and any talent must be developed.

Mastering the mind is like mastering a career or hobby, except the mind is with us twenty-four-seven. Learning a language takes time, regardless of who we are and what culture or ethnic background we are from.

Speaking a language with the perfect dialect takes much effort and experience. Similarly, we can master our minds with the same principles: *"Whoever is slow to anger has great understanding, but he who has a hasty temper exalts folly*" (Proverbs 14:29). The more effort we give, the less stressful we will be in the process. Everything in life takes time to master, like a language. The more we practice speaking it, the more fluent it becomes.

There are many thoughts that take up a lot of space in our brains, like squatters who do Qualifications not have permission to live in the location they choose. Some of our thoughts are there in our minds not because we have consciously given permission but because they came along due to past hurts.

The more they are fed with negativity, the more control they have, and eventually they rule the mind just like a squatter who will take over land or a residence they reside in. In order to take charge, make sure you are the one consciously permitting these thoughts to stay in your mind; otherwise, dispel them: *"Above all else, guard your heart, for everything you do flows from it"* (Proverbs 4:23).

There is usually a loose conglomeration of thoughts running through our minds that come from words spoken to us as children. It is often the case that these words take up space in our minds. These are usually thoughts that have us comparing ourselves with others, believing that we are useless, feeling that we will never succeed, or constantly in a state of trying to fulfill other people's expectations of us.

The conglomeration of thoughts that come from rejection and betrayal, which creates emotional pain, should be discarded ceremoniously, like putting an object that represents negativity in a box and burying or burning it. These are the thoughts that cripple us, and instead of being a master of our minds, we become a slave to them: *"Fear not, for I have redeemed you; I have called you by name, you are mine"* (Isaiah 43:1).

We should never allow our thoughts to make us feel like we are in bondage or like we are a slave to fear and worry: *"God has not given us a spirit of fear, but of power and of love and of a sound mind"* (2 Timothy 1:7 NKJV).

Anger, frustration, emotional pain, and regrets grow when we live in bondage. A lack of motivation, low self-esteem, insecurity, anxiety, depression, passivity, and violent behaviours are all signs that we may be in bondage due to our thoughts. Despite how much effect our thoughts can have on us, we are the masters of what we think: *"You will keep in perfect peace those whose minds are steadfast, because they trust in you"* (Isaiah 26:3).

We need to stop ourselves from thinking negatively. Start by saying to yourself, "I am in control." We can actually write it down or print on paper "I am in control" and paste it in places where it is visible to remind ourselves we are in charge of ourselves: *"I have been crucified with Christ and I no longer live, but Christ lives in me"* (Galatians 2:20). We should not blame others for our behaviours and actions.

We need to avoid beating ourselves up. It is okay to admit our flaws, weaknesses, faults, and regrets, but we need to move on: *"There is therefore now no condemnation for those who are in Christ Jesus"* (Romans 8:1).

Do not allow thoughts of self-disappointment to stay in your brain. No one can change what has happened; however, we can problem-solve. Therefore, looking for solutions instead of allowing negative thoughts to rule our minds should be our focus when things do not go the way we want them to. Sometimes we are our worst bullies. Do not allow your mind to bully you with negative thoughts: *"The Lord is merciful and gracious, slow to anger and abounding in steadfast love"* (Psalm 103:8).

Some unanswered questions that may help you and that are usually asked: "What are some tricks and pointers to becoming masters of your minds?" "How do we get rid of the slave mentality?" "How do we take charge of our thinking?"

Most of us need to change our attitude toward ourselves and others, at least at some point in our lives. We need to come to a place in life where we can conclude we do not have all the answers to all of life's problems, and we cannot "fix" others who may have wronged us.

Let that new positive attitude extend even to our enemies: "Love your enemies and pray for those who persecute you" (Matthew 5:44). When we start living in this fashion, we will grasp the basics of mastering our minds.

We should be alert to opportunities, realize that opportunities may never come again, and take advantage of them when they are in our hands: *"Making the best use of the time, because the days are evil"* (Ephesians 5:16 ESV).

We may fail, but that is a risk we will have to take. Each failure will draw us closer to the prize: *"I press on toward the goal to win the prize for which God has called me heavenward in Christ Jesus"* (Philippians 3:14). Opportunities will expand our experience and develop our skill set.

We need to accept people for who they are instead of trying to change them to be us. We all do our own assessment of people we meet and make a conscious decision to engage with them or maintain a distance. Accepting the fact that we cannot change anyone, but we can work with them, is another skill we need in order to master the mind: *"Accept one another, then, just as Christ accepted you"* (Romans 15:7).

A great deal of anxiety comes from feeling a lack of control when people do not behave how we want them to. Learning to accept others while being yourself and to let them make their own choices will have a positive impact on your relationship with them, which in turn will positively impact your outlook.

When we take responsibility, we set a different new example in life. We create a blueprint for others to follow: *"Each one should test their own actions. Then they can take pride in themselves alone, without comparing themselves to someone else"* (Galatians 6:4).

Regardless of what issues may arise as a result of our participation, we need to learn to take responsibility. We could be 100% right or 100% wrong, but we should take responsibility for finding a solution rather than blaming others. This shows maturity, but it is also a trick to allowing ourselves to learn that we are masters of our lives.

We need to ask ourselves why we sometimes live our lives more or less by ourselves and fail to include others. Where did it stem from? We can socialize and engage with others and not allow the power of influence to affect us negatively: "*Walk with the wise and become wise, for a companion of fools suffers harm*" (Proverbs 13:20).

We can be in control of our minds and what we think of ourselves and others without allowing fear to control us. We were created to be among others to help with healthy stimulants, which assist with preventative factors that will affect our mental health long term: "*And let us consider how we may spur one another on toward love and good deeds*" (Hebrews 10:24).

We need to maintain a mind of a student. Some of us may give the impression that we know it all and that we have an answer for everything in life, yet our own lives are falling apart. "*Pride goes before destruction, a haughty spirit before a fall*" (Proverbs 16:18).

When we are willing to learn, we will always be one step closer to mastering what we are learning: "*Let the wise hear and increase in learning*" (Proverbs 1:5 ESV). Assuming the role of a student allows for new thoughts to replace discarded thoughts as we stay in control of what we allow into our minds.

We also need to maintain a mind of a teacher. One thing observed from teaching is that it forces you to learn: "*Teach me your way, Lord, that I may rely on your faithfulness; give me an undivided heart*" (Psalm 86:11).

When we teach, experience and skills are sharpened. Find out how we can speak into the lives of others, even if it is our loved ones. The concept of centering our thoughts around communicating a theme will help us in taking control of our thought life.

When the brain is infected with lies, things can go awry. Our brain is a miracle in how it functions: "*I praise you because I am fearfully and wonderfully made*" (Psalm 139:14). We can become great servants to our minds if we fail to become masters over them.

Spend time concentrating and thinking through your thoughts before acting, forming opinions, or communicating opinions: "*Everyone should be quick to listen, slow to speak and slow to become angry*" (James 1:19).

We need to learn how to filter our thoughts if we want to master them: "*Finally, brothers and sisters, whatever is true, whatever is noble, whatever is right, whatever is pure, whatever is lovely, whatever is admirable—if anything is excellent or praiseworthy—think about such things*" (Philippians 4:8).

Mastering our minds draws us closer to the destinies assigned to us: "*For I know the plans I have for you," declares the Lord, "plans to prosper you and not to harm you, plans to give you hope and a future*" (Jeremiah 29:11).

We need to come to a place where we can master our minds. Otherwise, we will never be at peace with ourselves: "*You will keep in perfect peace those whose minds are steadfast*" (Isaiah 26:3).

If it is not good for you, cut it out; otherwise, it will become like cancer and can destroy you: "*Get rid of all bitterness, rage and anger… along with every form of malice*" (Ephesians 4:31).

We should never ignore our gut feeling. Many times the Holy Spirit speaks quietly before we feed a thought: "*Whether you turn to the right or to the left, your ears will hear a voice behind you, saying, 'This is the way; walk in it*'" (Isaiah 30:21). If you do not feel good about something, do not pursue it.

Learning to say no is okay: "*Simply let your 'Yes' be 'Yes,' and your 'No,' 'No'*" (Matthew 5:37). Learning to say no will help us stay focused on what is most important and keep us from being driven by impulsivity.

We need to control our assumptions: "*Do not judge by appearances, but judge with right judgment*" (John 7:24). We need to control planting negative thoughts, for they are like weeds: "*A heart at peace gives life to the body, but envy rots the bones*" (Proverbs 14:30).

Negativity feeds on your life and will draw joy from your heart. It is better to walk away and refocus your thoughts on what is healthy: *"Set your minds on things above, not on earthly things"* (Colossians 3:2).

We have the ability to be resilient: *"We are hard pressed on every side, but not crushed; perplexed, but not in despair... struck down, but not destroyed"* (2 Corinthians 4:8-9).

We are in control of our thoughts and can do whatever we put our minds to do with Christ: *"I can do all this through him who gives me strength"* (Philippians 4:13). We have more control over our thoughts than we may give ourselves credit for.

Mastering the mind gives us the power to be in control, especially when we remind ourselves that we do not have to give an answer to every question, we do not have to react to every emotion from others, we do not have to be impulsive, and that time is our best friend: *"Be still, and know that I am God"* (Psalm 46:10).

Mastering the mind is being able to weed out anything that may come across as harmful, demanding, questioning, parenting, and objective, so that we may live in the freedom and peace Christ purchased for us. In the next chapter we will be exploring "Restructuring the Mind" where you will learn about how to challenge some of things we think.

RESTRUCTURING

the MIND

Have you ever found yourself caught in a spiral of negative thoughts, where one small worry drags you into a storm of self-doubt? Perhaps you made a minor mistake at work and suddenly heard an inner voice insisting, "I always mess up. I'm hopeless at this job."

Or maybe an upcoming event filled you with dread, and thoughts like "I'm going to embarrass myself" or "I'm just not good enough" kept replaying until your whole body felt heavy.

I remember one evening, after a particularly difficult day, lying awake while my mind punished me for hours. My heart felt bruised, and I could almost feel the energy draining from me simply because of the weight of my own thoughts.

In those moments, I discovered a lifeline: restructuring my thoughts. This gentle practice, rooted in cognitive-behavioural therapy, is simply the art of noticing a thought, testing whether it is fully true, and then replacing it with something more balanced, kind, and grounded in reality.

It is not pretending everything is perfect; it is choosing to tell myself the truth in love (Ephesians 4:15). And it is one of the most practical ways I have ever lived out Romans 12:2: *"Do not conform to the pattern of this world, but be transformed by the renewing of your mind. Then you will be able to test and approve what God's will is—his good, pleasing and perfect will."*

The process is beautifully simple, yet it carries the power to change everything.

First, notice the thought. Most negative thoughts arrive automatically, like uninvited guests who have been visiting so long we no longer question their right to be there.

I once prepared for a presentation convinced I would humiliate myself. My stomach knotted, my palms sweated, and the sentence "Everyone will see I'm a failure" looped endlessly. Then, by God's grace, I paused and asked, "Where did that thought come from, and is it the whole truth?"

That single pause created a tiny gap of freedom—space enough for the Holy Spirit to enter. Psalm 139:23–24 became my prayer: *"Search me, God, and know my heart; test me and know my anxious thoughts. See if there is any offensive way in me, and lead me in the way everlasting."*

Second, gently challenge the thought. Ask for evidence, the way a kind lawyer would defend you in court. When I believed "I'm going to fail and everyone will laugh," I forced myself to list the facts: I had prepared thoroughly. I had received positive feedback on previous talks.

Colleagues had thanked me for helpful insights. The evidence did not support the terror. At that moment Isaiah 41:10 felt like a warm hand on my shoulder: *"So do not fear, for I am with you; do not be dismayed, for I am your God. I will strengthen you and help you; I will uphold you with my righteous right hand.*"

If the Creator of the universe says He will strengthen and uphold me, then surely I can trust that I am not as helpless as my fear insists.

Third, replace the old thought with a new one that is both true and compassionate. Instead of "I'm going to fail miserably," I began to say, "I might feel nervous, and that's okay—nerves mean I care. I am prepared, I am held by God, and whatever happens, my worth is secure in Him."

This is not toxic positivity; it is speaking the truth in love. Over time, these new sentences become the default soundtrack of my mind. As Proverbs 23:7 teaches, "*For as he thinks in his heart, so is he.*" What we rehearse in our hearts slowly becomes who we are.

Neuroscience confirms what Scripture declared long ago. Every time we notice, challenge, and replace a thought, we are engaging in deliberate neuroplasticity. The old neural pathway ("I'm a failure") loses strength through long-term depression in the amygdala, while the new pathway ("I am held, I am growing, I belong to God") is strengthened through long-term potentiation in the prefrontal cortex.

In the language of faith, we are putting off the old self and putting on the new (Ephesians 4:22–24), and God Himself is the Master Builder supervising the renovation.

This practice touches every corner of life. Anxiety softens because we stop pouring fuel on the fire of "what if." Depression lifts as we cease agreeing with the lie that we are worthless.

Relationships heal when we challenge thoughts like "They don't really care" and replace them with "I will choose to believe the best until proven otherwise" (1 Corinthians 13:7). Even our bodies respond—cortisol levels drop, sleep improves, energy returns—because we are no longer living under the constant inner warfare of self-condemnation.

I have leaned on many helpers along the way. Cognitive Processing Therapy taught me to unpack stuck beliefs from trauma. Dialectical Behaviour Therapy gave me skills to soothe overwhelming emotions. Mindfulness trained me to watch thoughts like clouds passing across the sky instead of mistaking them for the sky itself. Exposure therapy helped me face feared situations while whispering, *"The Lord is my light and my salvation—whom shall I fear?"* (Psalm 27:1).

And every time I sat with my wife Kathleen or my sister Annmarie, I felt like Aaron and Hur holding up Moses' arms—visible reminders that God often sends human hands to do His healing work.

Yet the most powerful moments happened alone with God and a simple journal. I began writing the negative thought on one side of the page and the evidence plus a Scripture on the other.

Some days the list was short and tear-stained; other days it filled pages. But every entry was a vote for truth. Philippians 4:8 became my daily filter: *"Whatever is true, whatever is noble, whatever is right, whatever is pure, whatever is lovely, whatever is admirable—if anything is excellent or praiseworthy—think about such things."* I learned to ask, "Is this thought true? Is it lovely? Is it praiseworthy?" If not, it did not deserve rent-free space in my mind.

Self-compassion is woven through it all. On days when the old thoughts roared back, I wrapped myself in Matthew 11:28–30: *"Come to me, all you who are weary and burdened, and I will give you rest... For my yoke is easy and my burden is light."* Jesus never scolds me for struggling; He invites me to bring the struggle to Him and rest while He does the heavy lifting.

Restructuring your thoughts is not a technique to master so you can feel better about yourself. It is an act of worship—an obedient response to the God who says, *"Let Me transform you by changing the way you think."*

Every time you notice a lie, challenge it with evidence and Scripture, and replace it with truth spoken in love, you are partnering with the Holy Spirit in the renewal of your mind. You are putting into practice 2 Corinthians 10:5—taking every thought captive to make it obedient to Christ.

Start small. Catch one thought. Write it down. Ask, "Is this the whole truth? What does God say?" Then speak His better word over yourself. Do it again tomorrow. And the next day. The garden of your mind will not change in a single afternoon, but every seed of truth you plant will grow.

And one day you will wake up and realize the weeds have been crowded out by flowers of peace, joy, and unshakable confidence in the love of your Father.

You are not stuck with the mind you have today. By the grace of God and the gift of a plastic, responsive brain, you are being transformed—gently, daily, wonderfully—into the likeness of Christ, who holds your mind in His scarred hands and whispers, "*Peace, be still*" (Mark 4:39). Keep going. The renewal has already begun.

Have you ever found yourself trapped in a spiral of negative thoughts, where one small fear drags you into a storm of despair? Perhaps you made a simple mistake and suddenly heard an inner voice declare, "You always ruin everything. You're hopeless." Or maybe an ordinary day turned dark because your mind insisted, "No one really loves you. You'll always be alone." God who specialises in breaking chains and renewing minds.

The Bible is full of people who learned to restructure their thoughts long before anyone coined the term "cognitive restructuring." Look at Gideon hiding in a winepress, convinced he was the least in the weakest clan (Judges 6:15). God called him "*mighty warrior*," and though Gideon argued at first, he finally began to speak and act according to God's truth instead of his fear. By the end, the man who once thought

"I'm nothing" led three hundred men to victory with nothing but trumpets and torches. His mind was renewed, and a nation was saved.

David knew the spiral too. In Psalm 42 he cried, "*Why, my soul, are you downcast? Why so disturbed within me*?"—and then, in the very same breath, he restructured his own thoughts: "*Put your hope in God, for I will yet praise him, my Savior and my God.*" David did this again and again in the psalms. He noticed the thought ("I'm alone, I'm sinking"), challenged it with truth ("Where does my help come from?"), and replaced it with worship ("My help comes from the Lord, the Maker of heaven and earth" – Psalm 121:1–2). David taught his soul a new song, and that new song carried him through caves, battles, and heartbreaking betrayal.

Peter is another beautiful example. After denying Jesus three times, he could easily have drowned in thoughts like "I'm a failure. I'm not worthy to be a disciple. I've ruined everything." Instead, on the shore of Galilee, Jesus met him with gentle questions and fresh commissioning (John 21:15–19). Peter allowed the Lord to replace "I'm the one who betrayed You" with "*You know I love You… Feed my sheep.*" From that moment, the man who once sank in fear walked on water again— this time in the power of a renewed mind—and preached at Pentecost until three thousand souls were added to the kingdom.

Even Paul, once the proud Pharisee Saul, had to restructure deeply ingrained thoughts. He had believed, "I am righteous by keeping the law perfectly." On the Damascus road Jesus shattered that lie, and Paul spent the rest of his life replacing it with "*I am the worst of sinners… but by the grace of God I am what I am*" (1 Timothy 1:15; 1 Corinthians 15:10). Every letter he wrote is evidence of a mind being daily renewed by grace.

These stories are not exceptions; they are invitations. The same God who renamed Gideon, retrained David's soul, restored Peter, and rewired Paul is ready to do it for us.

The process is still beautifully simple, and Scripture walks us through every step.

First, notice the thought. Elijah did this under the broom tree when despair said, *"It is enough; now, Lord, take my life"* (1 Kings 19:4). God didn't scold him; He fed him, let him sleep, and then spoke in a gentle whisper. Noticing the thought without shame is the beginning of freedom.

Second, challenge the thought with truth. When Satan tempted Jesus in the wilderness with lies—*"If you are the Son of God…"*—Jesus didn't debate feelings. Three times He answered, *"It is written"* (Matthew 4:1–11). He brought evidence from Deuteronomy straight into the desert of temptation. We can do the same. When the thought comes, "God has abandoned me," we answer with Hebrews 13:5: *"Never will I leave you; never will I forsake you."* When shame whispers, "You're too broken," we counter with Psalm 34:18: *"The Lord is close to the brokenhearted and saves those who are crushed in spirit."*

Third, replace the lie with God's living word spoken in love. This is what the prophet Jeremiah did in the darkest season of his life. Surrounded by ruin, he restructured his thoughts in Lamentations 3:19–23: *"I remember my affliction… yet this I call to mind and therefore I have hope: Because of the Lord's great love we are not consumed, for his compassions never fail. They are new every morning; great is your faithfulness."* From "It's hopeless" to "Great is Your faithfulness"—that single shift carried him through the fall of Jerusalem and still carries us today.

Neuroscience simply describes what God has always been doing. Every time we notice, challenge, and replace a thought, we are cooperating with the Holy Spirit in deliberate neuroplasticity. The old pathway weakens, the new pathway strengthens, and the God who *"makes everything new"* (Revelation 21:5) reshapes the very synapses of our brains with His truth.

I practice this almost every morning now. I sit with Kathleen, and we do devotions together reading the Word of God. I am usually with my coffee and my Bible and I name whatever fearful or shameful thought is trying to set the tone for the day.

Then I open the Word and let God speak the final word. Some mornings it's Isaiah 43:1: *"Fear not, for I have redeemed you; I have called you by name; you are mine."* Other mornings it's Zephaniah 3:17: *"The Lord your God is with you… He will take great delight in you… He will rejoice over you with singing."*

I write the verse creating a devotion which I share with all the children on a group chat and on social media. I carry it with me, and speak it aloud whenever the old thought tries to return. Little by little, the new truth becomes the native language of my mind.

You are not stuck with the thoughts that torment you today. Gideon was not stuck as the least in Manasseh. David was not stuck in despair. Peter was not stuck as the denier. Paul was not stuck as the persecutor. And you are not stuck either. The same God who met each of them in their spiral is meeting you right now, whispering, *"Let Me renew your mind. Let Me replace the lie with My truth. Let Me sing over you until you remember who you really are."*

Start small. Catch one thought today. Bring it to Jesus the way the bleeding woman reached for the hem of His garment (Mark 5:25–34). Let Him touch it, name it, heal it, and replace it with His better word. Then tomorrow, do it again.

The garden of your mind is being reclaimed, weed by weed, seed by seed, Scripture by Scripture. And one day soon you will lift your eyes and discover, with wonder and tears, that the voice you hear most clearly is no longer fear or shame, but the gentle, triumphant voice of the One who calls you beloved—and means it with all His heart.

TRAINING

the  MIND

Our thoughts play a vital role in shaping our mental abilities and performance. When we cultivate positive, organized, and structured thoughts, we enhance our cognitive functions and achieve far better results.

Have you ever sat down to study for an exam only to find your mind wandering to a hundred unrelated things? That happens because our thoughts have the power either to sharpen our focus or to scatter it completely.

A cluttered mind struggles to concentrate and retain information, while an orderly mind processes truth with clarity and strength. The Bible puts it plainly: *"For as he thinks in his heart, so is he"* (Proverbs 23:7). What we continually think eventually becomes who we are.

Note-taking works so well because it forces us to arrange ideas in an orderly way, and the very act of writing helps the brain lock information into long-term memory. Yet organization is only half the battle.

The content of our thoughts matters even more. Negative, self-limiting words act like poison to learning and growth. Tell yourself often enough, "I'm no good at this," and you will live out that lie. On the other hand, when we adopt the growth mindset God intends for His children—"I'm not able yet, but with practice and God's help I will improve"—we open the door to real progress. Paul urges us, *"Whatever things are true, whatever things are noble, whatever things are just, whatever things are pure... meditate on these things"* (Philippians 4:8).

Choosing to think on what is good is not mere optimism; it is obedience, and obedience always brings blessing.

The arrangement of our thoughts is crucial. Scattered thinking makes concentration almost impossible, but when thoughts are lined up systematically, mental clarity, memory, and problem-solving all improve dramatically.

Just as we train our bodies through exercise, we can train our brains through deliberate mental challenges. The process is lifelong and demands persistence, yet the rewards are more than worth the effort.

Learning a new language, tackling puzzles, playing memory games—any activity that stretches us beyond our comfort zone builds new neural pathways.

Scripture promises the same principle: *"Do not be conformed to this world, but be transformed by the renewing of your mind"* (Romans 12:2). Transformation is not a one-time event; it is daily renewal.

I used to break out in a cold sweat at the sight of numbers. In fact when I was studying for my doctorate degree in clinical psychology, I had to get a tutor. Math had tormented me since grade school.

A few years ago I started playing Sudoku every evening. At first it frustrated me to tears, but I refused to quit. Week after week I persisted, and something remarkable happened: the same brain that once froze during simple equations began to see patterns quickly and accurately.

My anxiety melted away, and I actually started enjoying numbers. My story is living proof that "*if anyone is in Christ, he is a new creation*" (2 Corinthians 5:17)—even in the way we think.

We all have those embarrassing moments when we forget a name two seconds after being introduced or walk into a room and completely blank on why we came. Instead of shrugging it off, try simple memory games—matching pairs, word associations, recalling lists.

At first it feels pointless, but daily practice produces undeniable improvement. I love what God told Joshua on the edge of the Promised Land: "*This Book of the Law shall not depart from your mouth, but you shall meditate in it day and night... for then you will make your way prosperous, and then you will have good success*" (Joshua 1:8). Daily meditation on God's Word is the ultimate memory exercise, and it never returns void.

Training the brain reaches far beyond better grades or job performance. Sharpened focus helps us study, work, and create with excellence. Trained creativity produces fresh solutions and beautiful expressions of worship.

A disciplined thought life calms anxiety and lifts depression because we learn to "*cast all your care upon Him, for He cares for you*" (1 Peter 5:7) instead of carrying the burden alone.

Confidence and healthy self-esteem are not pride; they are the fruit of knowing whose we are. When we grasp that we are "*fearfully and wonderfully made*" (Psalm 139:14), we walk into rooms—interviews, friendships, opportunities—with quiet assurance.

Good communication flows from a well-trained mind. James warns that the tongue is a small member but boasts great things and can set a whole life on fire (James 3:5-6).

Learning to pause, pray, and choose words carefully saves marriages, restores friendships, and opens doors that harshness would slam shut. A sharp memory keeps us organized and faithful in small things, which the Lord says is preparation for ruling cities (Luke 16:10).

Clear decision-making is simply wisdom applied, and *"the fear of the Lord is the beginning of wisdom"* (Proverbs 9:10). Every area of life improves when we learn to direct our thinking instead of letting it direct us.

Science confirms what Scripture declared: regular mental exercise lowers the risk of cognitive decline, lifts mood, reduces stress, and increases overall well-being.

God designed our brains to grow when we use them. So find something that challenges you—learn an instrument, pick up a new language, master chess, memorize Scripture—and practice faithfully. *"Whatever you do, do it heartily, as to the Lord"* (Colossians 3:23).

Mind maps have become one of my favourite tools. Draw a central idea in the middle of a page and let branches flow outward with every related thought, colour, or verse that comes to mind.

Suddenly chaos becomes clarity, and the big picture and fine details sit peacefully side by side. It is a visible picture of what Paul prayed for the Ephesians: that God would give them *"the spirit of wisdom and revelation"* and enlighten *"the eyes of their understanding"* (Ephesians 1:17-18).

Journaling is quiet therapy with the Holy Spirit. When I pour out my heart on paper—fears, gratitude, confession, dreams—I see patterns I missed while everything swirled inside my head. David wrote, *"When I kept silent, my bones grew old through my groaning all the day long"* (Psalm 32:3). Bringing thoughts into the light brings healing and order.

Meditation is not emptying the mind but filling it with truth. Ten quiet minutes breathing slowly while repeating *"Be still, and know that I am God"* (Psalm 46:10) can reset an entire day.

Positive self-talk is simply agreeing with what God has already said about us: *"I can do all things through Christ who strengthens me"* (Philippians 4:13).

Gratitude rewires the brain to notice blessing instead of lack; it is why Paul commands us to *"give thanks in all circumstances"* (1 Thessalonians 5:18).

Keep learning. The moment we decide we know enough, the brain begins to coast downhill. Pick up a new hobby, read widely, ask questions. *"Wise people store up knowledge"* (Proverbs 10:14).

And never forget the body God gave you—good food, movement, and sleep are not extras; they are part of the care of the temple of the Holy Spirit (1 Corinthians 6:19-20).

Training your mind is not a one-time event; it is a lifestyle of daily renewal. When thoughts are brought captive to Christ (2 Corinthians 10:5), stress loses its grip, relationships deepen, purpose sharpens, and joy multiplies.

You feed your mind every day—through conversations, media, music, and thoughts. Choose life-giving input, because *"a man is what he thinks about all day long."* Guard your heart and mind with all diligence, for from them flow the wellsprings of life (Proverbs 4:23).

Start small today. One verse memorized. One gratitude list. One puzzle finished. One kind word spoken to yourself. The same Spirit who raised Jesus from the dead is ready to quicken your mortal body and renew your mind. Step by step, thought by thought, you are becoming the person God already sees—confident, clear-minded, compassionate, and unstoppable—because your mind is being transformed into the image of Christ.

I used to think my brain was simply the way God made me—scattered, anxious, and prone to forgetting everything. I accepted it the way some people accept bad knees or a slow metabolism.

Then one winter afternoon everything changed. I was in my early fifty's, standing in the middle of my kitchen holding a jar of peanut butter, crying because I couldn't remember whether I had paid a bill. I was studying for my second doctorate degree. One of my daughter looked up at me with her big dark brown eyes and asked, "Dad, are you okay?" I wasn't. That was the day I decided my brain was not my master; it was my student, and school was now in session.

The first thing I did was the simplest and the hardest: I started waking up an hour earlier before everyone else. In that quiet hour I did three things without fail. I read one chapter of the Bible slowly, out loud. I wrote down whatever fear or lie was loudest in my head and then answered it with a verse I looked up. And I did ten minutes of Lumosity or a Sudoku puzzle, or candy crush on my phone. Nothing fancy, nothing expensive—just consistency.

Six weeks in, Kathleen noticed first. "You're not snapping at the kids as much," she said. I laughed and told her I was too mentally tired from brain games to have energy left for yelling.

A few months later I faced a bigger test. I was asked to speak at a women's conference in Sudbury—three or four hundred women attending. Public speaking has always been my hobby, however I was concerned that my mind would go blank, my palms would sweat, and I would forget my own name.

I've learned that a trained brain doesn't just help you—it helps everyone your life touches.

Memory work became my secret love language with Jesus. There is something intimate about carrying His words inside you. During a season of depression, I felt it tried to swallow me whole, I read the entire book of Philippians—one verse a day, sometimes one verse a week when the darkness was thick.

On the nights when I couldn't sleep because my mind was screaming lies, I would lie in bed and recite Paul's words: "***Rejoice in the Lord always. Again I will say, rejoice!***" Over and over until my heartbeat slowed and peace came. Doctors can prescribe medicine (and I'm grateful for it), but only the living Word can reach the places pills can't touch.

Even physical exercise became brain training. I discovered that a twenty-minute walk while praying in tongues or quoting Scripture does more for my mental clarity than an extra hour of sleep some days.

The most recent adventure is language. I'm learning Spanish at fifty-seven, slowly and badly, with Duolingo and social media. Last month I had a dream entirely in Spanish. I woke up laughing because my brain—my old, tired, anxiety-riddled brain—had done something it never could have done a decade ago.

Here's what I know now that I didn't know then: your brain is not fixed. It is fearfully and wonderfully made, yes, but it is also renewable, day by day. Every time you choose to memorize a verse instead of scroll, to solve a puzzle instead of numb out, to speak kindly to yourself instead of critically, you are laying down a new pathway. You are proving to your own soul that "I am being transformed by the renewing of my mind."

I still forget things from time to time. I still have anxious days. I still feel like a confused goldfish. But those moments no longer define me. They are just reminders that training is never finished this side of heaven. And every single day I get to wake up and choose again: Will I let my thoughts run me, or will I take them captive and teach them to sit at Jesus' feet?

Start today. One verse. One puzzle. One kind word to yourself. One prayer walked out on a quiet park. The transformation won't happen overnight, but it will happen one obedient thought at a time. And one day you will look back, like I do now, and realize the scared, scattered person you used to be is almost unrecognizable—because you dared to believe that with God, all things really are possible, even a brand-new mind.

FEEDING

the MIND

"Guard your heart with all diligence, for out of it spring the issues of life" (Proverbs 4:23). The writer of Proverbs knew long before modern neuroscience that whatever you allow to pass through the gate of your mind will eventually settle in your heart and flow out into your life.

Today we call this "brain feeding"—the deliberate choice of what thoughts, words, images, conversations, and truths we allow to nourish our minds every single day.

I learned this the hard way. After our twins were born, I fell into the habit of scrolling social media. I told myself it was harmless—ten minutes of seeing people make a fool of themselves and funny memes went into a hour. Night after night I was feeding my exhausted brain a steady diet of comparison, outrage, and perfectionism disguised as inspiration.

Within weeks I was convinced I was failing at everything: my body wasn't bouncing back fast enough, my tasks weren't being completed, my time with Kathleen and the children weren't memorable. In fact when I look back at some videos the children took during family events, I was always on my phone. I even fell asleep with my phone.

One morning I caught myself getting upset because there were so many things to get done around the house. That was the day I realized my mind was literally malnourished. I was feeding it junk food and wondering why I woke up anxious and depleted.

So I made a rule that still stands in our house today: nothing enters my eyes or ears before something good enters my spirit. I started keeping my Bible and a gratitude journal in my home office instead of my phone.

What we feed on is what we become. Jesus said, *"The good man out of the good treasure of his heart brings forth what is good… for his mouth speaks from that which fills his heart"* (Luke 6:45). Your heart is a treasury, and your mind is the doorkeeper.

Every song lyric, every news headline, every conversation, every thought you entertain is making a deposit into that treasury.

I saw the opposite play out a few years ago with a close friend. He was going through a painful divorce and began listening to angry music, reading bitter forums, and watching shows filled with revenge and betrayal.

At first he said it "helped him process," but month after month the bitterness grew roots. He became sharp, suspicious, and hopeless. One day he looked at me with tears in his eyes and said, "I don't recognize myself anymore." We sat together at a coffee shop, opened Philippians 4:8—*"Whatever is true, whatever is honorable, whatever is just, whatever is pure… think on these things"*—and made a new plan.

For thirty days he replaced every angry song with worship, every bitter post with Scripture, every revenge show with something beautiful or funny. Thirty days later he told me, "I feel like I've been detoxing my soul." He had been. He was learning that you cannot feast on poison and expect to stay healthy.

Positivity is not pretending problems don't exist; it is choosing to fix your mind on what is true. When we feed on gratitude, Scripture, beauty, and truth, the brain actually changes.

Neurochemicals like dopamine and serotonin increase, stress hormones decrease, blood pressure lowers, and the immune system strengthens. Paul knew this when he wrote, *"Rejoice always... in everything give thanks; for this is the will of God in Christ Jesus for you"* (1 Thessalonians 5:16-18). Gratitude is brain food straight from heaven.

Negativity is slow spiritual suicide. It activates the body's stress response, floods us with cortisol, and literally shrinks the parts of the brain responsible for memory and emotional regulation.

I learned this personally when I went through a season of watching the news obsessively during an election year. I told myself I was "staying informed," but I was actually marinating in fear and division. My sleep suffered, my prayers turned angry, and I started seeing enemies everywhere.

One day the Holy Spirit whispered, *"Do everything without complaining or arguing, so that you may become blameless and pure"* (Philippians 2:14-15). I turned the news off and replaced it with the Gospels. Days and months later I was calmer, kinder, and—honestly—much better informed about what actually mattered.

Protecting your mind is not weakness; it is wisdom. David prayed, *"Set a guard, O Lord, over my mouth; keep watch over the door of my lips"* (Psalm 141:3). I pray a version of that over my eyes and ears now:

Lord, be the doorkeeper of my mind. Nothing gets past You that will harm me.

Here are the practical ways I feed my brain every single day, and I promise they work because I am living proof:

1. First thing in the morning, start the day with worship music. Have a song on repeat if it is speaking life into you. Let your house be filled with songs that exalt Jesus. My children grew up thinking every home naturally sounds like heaven in the morning.

2. Scripture before screen. Read the scripture loud and one psalm. Speaking truth audibly is powerful—there's a reason God told Joshua to meditate on the Word day and night and to keep it on his lips (Joshua 1:8).

3. Gratitude out loud. I thank God for five specific things before my feet leave the house. "*This is the day the Lord has made; I will rejoice and be glad in it*" (Psalm 118:24) is my daily declaration.

4. Movement with truth. I walk or run almost every day while listening to the Bible or preaching that builds faith. "*Faith comes by hearing, and hearing by the word of God*" (Romans 10:17)—even at mile three.

5. Beauty on purpose. Fresh flowers on the table, candles at dinner, art on the walls, birdsong through open windows. God created a world dripping with glory; beholding it feeds the soul.

6. People who speak life. I protect time with friends who leave me feeling built up, not torn down. "*Walk with the wise and become wise*" (Proverbs 13:20).

7. Limited, intentional media. I have set times for news and social media, and I unfollow anything or anyone that stirs envy, anger, or fear. My peace is worth more than being "up to date."

8. Creativity as worship. I write, garden, play piano—anything that lets me co-create with God. He is the ultimate Creator, and

making things with our hands reminds us we are made in His image.

9. Laughter every day. My family is loud and ridiculous on purpose. *"A merry heart does good, like medicine"* (Proverbs 17:22).

10. Early bedtime with a good book. Nothing dark, nothing disturbing—just stories and truths that settle my spirit for rest.

Feeding your brain is not a luxury; it is spiritual warfare in its gentlest form. Every choice to read Scripture instead of gossip, to worship instead of worry, to laugh instead of complain, is an act of taking ground for the Kingdom inside your own soul.

Friend, you have more control than you think. You get to choose today—and every day—what you will allow past the gate of your mind. Feed it life. Feed it truth. Feed it beauty. Feed it Jesus. Because whatever you feed will grow, and one day soon you will wake up and discover that the peace you longed for, the joy you prayed for, the resilience you needed, has been growing inside you all along—quietly, faithfully, one good thought at a time.

"Finally, brethren, whatever things are true, whatever things are noble, whatever things are just, whatever things are pure, whatever things are lovely, whatever things are of good report, if there is any virtue and if there is anything praiseworthy—meditate on these things… and the God of peace will be with you" (Philippians 4:8-9). That is a promise you can feast on for the rest of your life.

Brain feeding is not a cute metaphor. It is a biological, neurological, and deeply spiritual reality. What you feed your brain literally becomes the material from which your thoughts, emotions, memories, reactions, and even your physical health are built.

Every second you are awake, your brain is taking in information through your five senses and deciding what to do with it. This process is called neuroplasticity: your brain is plastic, moldable, constantly rewiring itself based on what it experiences most. Neurons that fire together wire together. The pathways that get the most traffic become superhighways. The ones that get no traffic become overgrown and eventually disappear.

When you watch a thirty-minute reel of political rage, your amygdala (the fear center) lights up, cortisol floods your bloodstream, and your brain strengthens the neural pathway labeled "people are the enemy." Do that every evening for a month and your brain literally reshapes itself to scan for threats first and fastest. You will feel anxious even when nothing is wrong because your brain is simply doing the job you trained it to do.

Now flip the input. When you spend thirty minutes reading Psalm 23 out loud, thanking God for specific blessings, or listening to worship music, a completely different process begins. Your prefrontal cortex (the thinking, planning, faith center) lights up. Dopamine and serotonin are released. Oxytocin (the love and bonding hormone) increases.

The neural pathway labeled "God is good and He is with me" gets widened and strengthened. Do that every morning for a month and your brain rewires itself to scan for evidence of God's presence first. You will wake up calmer, kinder, and braver—even when circumstances haven't changed—because your brain is doing the job you trained it to do.

God is not asking you to try harder with the same broken wiring. He is inviting you to let Him rewire the entire house, room by room, thought by thought, feeding by feeding.

The single greatest predictor of happiness and health in old age is not money, fame, or even exercise. It's the quality of our relationships— what we chose to think about the people closest to us. Bitter, critical thoughts produced bitter, critical people. Grateful, generous thoughts produced grateful, generous people. Same circumstances. Different feeding. Different lives.

I found when we write down three things we are grateful for every night for three weeks, there is a measurable increases in happiness and decreases in depression symptoms that lasted six months later. Our brains literally grown new pathways of joy.

You are not a victim of your thoughts. You are the gardener of your mind. Every day you get to choose: Will I plant thorns or fruit? Will I water weeds or flowers? Will I feed fear or faith?

I am living proof that a frightened, angry, overwhelmed man can become calm, kind, and unshakable—not because circumstances got easier, but because I changed what I was feeding my brain every single day.

Put your phone across the room. Open your Bible. Thank God out loud for three impossible things that are still true: He is good. He is with you. He is not finished. Then go to sleep with those truths echoing in the hallways of your mind.

`The garden of your mind is waiting, and the Master Gardener has already given you everything you need to make it bloom. Feed it life, Feed it Jesus. And watch what grows.

COACHING

the

Are you sick of feeling stuck or not wanting to do anything? Do you have trouble with negative thoughts or doubts about yourself? If so, it's time to train your mind and take charge of your feelings and thoughts. *"We tear down arguments and anything that goes against the knowledge of God, and we make every thought obey Christ"* (2 Corinthians 10:5).

To coach our brains, we need to change the way we think so that we can overcome problems and reach our goals. Romans 12:2 says, *"Do not conform to the pattern of this world, but be transformed by the renewing of your mind."*

Coaching your brain can help you reach your goals, whether they are to do better at work, have better relationships, or feel more confident and happy. It is the art of teaching your brain to think positively and logically. Philippians 4:8 says, "*Whatever is true, whatever is noble, whatever is right, whatever is pure, whatever is lovely, whatever is admirable—if anything is excellent or praiseworthy—think about such things.*"

Instead of letting our minds control us, we need to work on them and become the master of our minds. Proverbs 14:30 says, "*A heart at peace gives life to the body.*"

This means that a healthy mind can lead to a healthy body, healthy relationships, and a happy life. We need to train our brains because it is important for healing the mind. When we go through emotional pain or trauma, our brains and bodies can get stuck in cycles of negative thoughts and feelings that are hard to break out of.

We can learn to see and deal with these patterns in a better way by training our minds. Philippians 4:7 says, "*The peace of God, which transcends all understanding, will guard your hearts and your minds in Christ Jesus.*"

You can get rid of all kinds of physical pain... Like the psalmist who said, "*When anxiety was great within me, your consolation brought joy to my soul*" (Psalm 94:19), using visualization and relaxation techniques on a regular basis will calm your nervous system and ease your pain.

Coaching our brains could change everything... We can use our body's natural healing powers and feel better and more alive by learning how to control our thoughts and feelings in a more positive way. As Isaiah 40:31 says, "*those who hope in the LORD will renew their strength.*"

Our mind is the greatest gift we have, but it can also be a curse if it gets out of control and starts to control us. "*Above all else, guard your heart, for everything you do flows from it*" (Proverbs 4:23).

Meditation (Joshua 1:8), being mindful of God's presence, and cognitive-behavioural therapy principles that fit with "*casting all your anxiety on him because he cares for you*" (1 Peter 5:7) are just a few of the cool ways to coach our brains.

Meditation is a way to train your mind to stay in the present... "*I think about your ways and meditate on your precepts*" (Psalm 119:15).

It's about learning to accept and deal with your thoughts and feelings in a good way instead of trying to push them away or ignore them. Psalm 139:23–24 says, "*Search me, God, and know my heart; test me and know my anxious thoughts.*"

You might also be trying to start a new workout plan... Celebrate small victories: "*His mercies begin anew each morning*" (Lamentations 3:23).

Imagining things is also helpful... Picture yourself reaching your goals, just like the Bible says: "*No eye has seen, no ear has heard... what God has prepared for those who love him*" (1 Corinthians 2:9).

Talking to yourself in a good way... Say, "*I am fearfully and wonderfully made*" (Psalm 139:14) and "*I am God's workmanship, created in Christ Jesus for good works*" (Ephesians 2:10) instead of "I'm not good enough."

Give thanks. "*Give thanks in all situations; this is God's will for you in Christ Jesus.*" (1 Thessalonians 5:18).

When we train our brains, we can understand and identify our thoughts and feelings... We can begin to recognize any negative patterns or beliefs that may be holding us back by being more mindful. "*See if there is any offensive way in me, and lead me in the way everlasting*" (Psalm 139:24).

The health of our minds, bodies, and emotions all depend on each other... Take care of yourself... "*Come to me, all you who are tired and heavy-laden, and I will give you rest*" (Matthew 11:28).

To have a growth mindset, you need to see problems as chances to learn and grow. "*Consider it pure joy when you go through all kinds of trials, because you know that the testing of your faith makes you stronger"* (James 1:2–3).

We can't teach our minds in just one day, that's for sure. Brain coaching is a process that never ends... *"being changed into his image with ever-increasing glory"* (2 Corinthians 3:18).

And believe me, every second you spend training your brain will be worth it... *"Don't get tired of doing good; if you don't give up, you will reap a harvest at the right time"* (Galatians 6:9).

Coaching our brains can also make us more productive and motivated... *"May the God of hope fill you with all joy and peace as you trust in him, so that you may overflow with hope by the power of the Holy Spirit"* (Romans 15:13).

We automatically become more powerful and free when we coach our brains. We are in charge of our own lives because of God's sovereign grace, and we are happier overall—*"It is for freedom that Christ has set us free"* (Galatians 5:1).

So, if you want to live your best life, you need to renew your mind every day (Romans 12:2), take every thought captive (2 Corinthians 10:5), focus on what is true and lovely (Philippians 4:8), and let the peace of Christ rule in your heart (Colossians 3:15). You don't have to stay stuck in your mind. With Christ, it can change in a steady, wonderful way.

DECLUTTERING

the MIND

Our brains are very strong. They're one of the best things God has given us: *"I praise you because I am fearfully and wonderfully made; your works are wonderful, I know that full well"* (Psalm 139:14).

But if we don't use our minds correctly or don't take care of them, things can get pretty bad. We always have thoughts in our heads that could be good or bad, and these thoughts shape the way we see things. These things are everything we can feel with our five senses, like our relationships, friends and family, jobs, and our self-image and self-worth.

Sometimes, we get too many thoughts that are too negative, racy, uncontrollable, and completely unnecessary.

At this point, our ability to think clearly goes to sleep, leaving us with a noisy, hurt, and congested mind that is going to burn out or catch fire.

Don't worry, just relax and take a deep breath. You have some good news: "*You will keep in perfect peace those whose minds are steadfast, because they trust in you*" (Isaiah 26:3).

Our minds are sensitive and fragile, and what we eat, see, hear, and do can all affect them. But God has given this amazing body organ a lot of strength and endurance.

Our brain has a godlike ability to control both our voluntary and involuntary actions. Our brain is still here to help us and control the functions of our other important organs, like the heart, even when we are under a lot of stress and pressure.

A mind has the ability to think in different ways, which means it can come up with a lot of new ideas and solutions to problems that seem impossible at first. We need to let our thoughts flow freely and not let them take over us if we want to unlock this god-mode of our brains.

We need to be in charge of our thoughts, or they will be in charge of us: "*We take captive every thought to make it obedient to Christ*" (2 Corinthians 10:5).

If we don't, we'll end up with negative thoughts that make us think in ways that aren't helpful or healthy. So, we need to change the way we think, take charge of what we do, and do it better: "*Do not conform to the pattern of this world, but be transformed by the renewing of your mind*" (Romans 12:2).

Brain damage doesn't happen all at once, and brain healing doesn't happen overnight. To reach the peak of productivity, we need to take small, effective steps to unlock our potential.

Let's start this healing journey with the simplest but most effective method, which is called "Decluttering." To declutter means to get rid of things or information that aren't needed or wanted in order to make a space or life more organized and simple.

Decluttering can be done in more than just your mind. It can also be done in physical spaces like homes, offices, and cars, as well as digital spaces like email accounts and computer desktops.

It can also mean cutting back on the number of things you have to do every day so you can focus on what matters most: *"Set your minds on things above, not on earthly things"* (Colossians 3:2).

Getting rid of clutter can help you feel less stressed, more productive, and more calm and clear. Setting clear goals and making a plan of action can help you declutter more effectively.

This could mean going through each area of a space in a planned way and putting things into groups, like "keep," "donate," and "throw away." It can also help to regularly go over and reevaluate the things or commitments in your life to keep clutter from building up again.

We declutter our minds and brains in the same way. It would not be inaccurate to assert that decluttering constitutes the most pragmatic and fundamental step in cognitive recovery.

Brain decluttering is the act of getting rid of thoughts and information that aren't useful or necessary in order to boost focus, productivity, and mental health.

It means putting our thoughts in order, getting rid of thoughts that are distracting or negative, and making room in our minds to focus on the present and important tasks: *"Finally, brothers and sisters, whatever is true, whatever is noble, whatever is right, whatever is pure, whatever is lovely, whatever is admirable—if anything is excellent or praiseworthy—think about such things"* (Philippians 4:8).

It's very important to clear our minds because it can help us get rid of all those annoying thoughts and distractions that make it hard to focus on what's really important.

When our brains are full of junk, it can also make us feel stressed and anxious, which is not cool at all. So, if we take some time to clear our minds, we can focus better, feel less stressed, and just feel better in general.

Some days in our lives, we have a lot on our minds. We think about work, our personal lives, and all the little things that seem to add up and make us very stressed all the time.

In these situations, we often feel tired and overwhelmed because it's hard for us to focus on one thing for too long. The answer to this problem is "decluttering," which is a sure way to solve it.

It's hard to concentrate on what you're doing when your mind is full of useless thoughts and distractions. These groups of unrelated thoughts and mental distractions can make you feel stressed and anxious, and even give you the feeling of mental fog.

This is not the end of it. It's hard to make good choices and pick what's best for us when our minds are full of things. It can stop us from being creative and make it harder for us to think of new ideas.

We could easily get overwhelmed and anxious because we have so many thoughts going through our heads. This would make it hard for us to remember important details and information.

In short, we can't work, think, sleep, make decisions, solve problems, or enjoy our lives when our minds are full of too many thoughts or when we're always thinking about a lot of things at once.

And we need to stop it early on, or we might unknowingly put ourselves at risk for serious mental illnesses like Generalized Anxiety Disorder (GAD), Major Depressive Disorder, ADHD, and many others.

There are days when it seems like we have a million things on our minds. It can be hard to concentrate on anything when there is so much stuff around. That's where decluttering comes in. We can get more done and be more productive if we take the time to clear our heads and organize our thoughts.

We can also focus on the thoughts that matter and get it done on time and more quickly. So, if you feel like your mind is full of junk and you're not getting as much done as you should, try decluttering. It might be the only way to reach your full potential! We can also make better decisions by decluttering our minds.

When we have unresolved thoughts and confused thinking patterns, it's hard to make good decisions. We can think more clearly, weigh our options, and make better decisions if we clear our minds: "*Trust in the Lord with all your heart and lean not on your own understanding; in all your ways submit to him, and he will make your paths straight*" (Proverbs 3:5-6).

Decluttering has magical effects that go beyond making you more productive and better at making decisions. The amazing technique of brain decluttering can help us be more creative. An overstuffed mind can't work right and also hurts our imagination.

But when we clear our minds, we can make room for new ideas and ways of doing things, which helps us tap into our creative side: "*Now to him who is able to do immeasurably more than all we ask or imagine, according to his power that is at work within us*" (Ephesians 3:20).

The importance of decluttering the brain doubles because it helps us feel calmer and more grounded and reduces feelings of stress, anxiety, and depression. We can learn to focus on one important task, which will help us remember things better and concentrate better.

And organizing our thoughts before bed can help us relax and get ready for a good night's sleep. Taking the time to clear your mind can help you become more aware of your thoughts and how you think.

Being aware of yourself can help you find and change negative thought patterns, boost your emotional intelligence, and even make you healthier.

In general, clearing out our brains can be good for our mental and emotional health, as well as our creativity and productivity. It is important for getting better at concentrating, lowering stress, clearing your mind, and being more productive and creative.

And by making it a habit, we can help ourselves a lot by improving our ability to think clearly, make good choices, and live the focused, happy life we've always wanted: *"For I know the plans I have for you," declares the Lord, "plans to prosper you and not to harm you, plans to give you hope and a future"* (Jeremiah 29:11).

Brain decluttering is not difficult, and anyone can do it at home. But the benefits it gives you are second to none, and they are like therapy from a doctor who has been doing it for a long time.

We can do simple things to improve our mental health. There are many ways to clear your mind, such as writing things down or practicing mindfulness. It's important to find a way that works for you and make it a habit. This will help you get through your to-do list more easily and feel less stressed in general.

Don't worry if you feel like your mind is too cluttered and overwhelmed and you don't want to do "fancy" things that might help clear your mind. We can start this journey of healing by taking a break from everything we need to do.

Taking a break from the chaos for a little while can sometimes help you clear your mind. Stop working, using your phone, or doing anything else that is making you anxious or stressed.

Take a few deep breaths and try to clear your head. Find a quiet spot, sit down, close your eyes, and pay attention to your breathing. When your mind starts to wander, gently bring your focus back to your breath: *"Be still before the Lord and wait patiently for him"* (Psalm 37:7).

To keep our minds healthy, we should also take care of our bodies. Exercise or physical activity is good for our bodies and can also help us think more clearly. Our brains release endorphins when we work out, which are chemicals that make us feel better. Also, exercise can help lower stress and anxiety, which can make your brain feel cluttered. And we can do anything we like, like running, swimming, walking, or even dancing: "Offer your bodies as a living sacrifice, holy and pleasing to God" (Romans 12:1).

If your bedroom, wardrobe, or work desk is messy, or if your bedroom is all over the place, don't expect your mind to work the way we want it to. Spend some time cleaning up your home and work space. Organize the things you still have and get rid of the things you don't need or use anymore. A clean space can help you feel calm and clear: *"Let all things be done decently and in order"* (1 Corinthians 14:40).

The main goal of brain decluttering is to put the most important tasks at the top of your list. It can be hard to do everything at once when we have a lot to do. Making a to-do list and figuring out which tasks are the most important can help us focus and think clearly.

Do the most important things first, and then move on to the less important ones: *"Seek first his kingdom and his righteousness, and all these things will be given to you as well"* (Matthew 6:33).

We can boost our productivity and clear our minds by breaking our work into smaller, more manageable pieces. And don't forget to take breaks. You should give your brain a break every now and then. Taking breaks can help you think more clearly and stay focused. Go for a short walk, read a book, or do something else that makes you happy. When you go back to work, you might be more focused and productive.

Brain decluttering will help you relax, boost your productivity, and improve your mental health. We need to get enough sleep for the brain decluttering to work best. Sleep is important for both your body and mind. Not getting enough sleep can make our brains cluttered and make it harder for us to focus: *"In peace I will lie down and sleep, for you alone, Lord, make me dwell in safety"* (Psalm 4:8).

So, we should go to bed and wake up at the same time every night and get enough sleep. If you have trouble falling asleep, do something relaxing before bed, like read a book or take a warm bath.

We shouldn't forget about the power of gratitude along with sleep. Being grateful for the good things in our lives is what gratitude is all about. We can clear our minds and feel better by focusing on what we have and who we are: *"Give thanks in all circumstances; for this is God's will for you in Christ Jesus"* (1 Thessalonians 5:18).

So, every day, take some time to think about what you're thankful for, like your health, your relationships, or the little things that make life better. Being thankful can help us feel more centered and grounded.

WEEDING

the MIND

Weeding is a common term in gardening. Weeding is the act of removing unwanted plants, such as weeds, from a garden or flower bed. People often don't want weeds because they can steal sunlight, water, and nutrients from other plants. If you don't keep an eye on them, weeds can grow quickly and take over a flower bed or garden. This can hurt other plants and make it hard for them to grow.

In the same way, "weeding" can mean finding and getting rid of bad or unhelpful thoughts or habits in your mind. Like weeds can take over a garden and hurt other plants, negative thoughts or habits can take over our minds and hurt our mental health: *"**Finally, brothers and sisters, whatever is true, whatever is noble, whatever is right, whatever is pure, whatever is lovely, whatever is admirable—if anything is excellent or praiseworthy—think about such things**"* (Philippians 4:8).

"Brain weeding" is a new word, and not much is known about where it came from. But many cultures have been doing things to clear their minds for hundreds of years. The idea of clearing your mind of clutter has been around for a long time and is common in many cultures: "***Do not conform to the pattern of this world, but be transformed by the renewing of your mind***" (Romans 12:2).

People have been talking more about "brain weeding" in the last few years as a way to deal with all the information and distractions in their lives. A lot of people do it now to help them think more clearly, stay on task, and feel better overall.

In Eastern philosophies, meditation is a common way to clear the mind and make it easier to think clearly.

Another way to weed your brain is to practice mindfulness, which means being aware of the present moment and accepting your thoghts and feelings without judging them: "***You will keep in perfect peace those whose minds are steadfast, because they trust in you***" (Isaiah 26:3).

Brain weeding is like minimalism in the West. Minimalism is the idea that you can make your life easier by getting rid of things that are cluttering your mind and body. Minimalism tells people to get rid of things they don't need and pay attention to the things they do need: "***Set your minds on things above, not on earthly things***" (Colossians 3:2).

Being aware of negative self-talk, like "I'm not good enough" or "I'll never be able to do that," and replacing it with more positive self-talk, like "I'm capable and worthy of success" or "I can learn and grow with practice," is what brain weeding is all about.

We can be happier and healthier by getting rid of these bad thoughts and replacing them with better ones: "***We take captive every thought to make it obedient to Christ***" (2 Corinthians 10:5).

To weed our minds, we need to find bad or unhelpful thoughts and habits and replace them with better ones. You can do this by practicing cognitive-behavioural therapy, meditation, mindfulness, or just taking the time to think about what you do and how you can do it better.

For example, learning a new skill, like playing the guitar, can be very hard. But every time you try to practice, you get angry and think, "I'll never be able to play like a pro." If you talk to yourself negatively, it can keep you from making progress and make it hard to stay motivated and focused on your goal.

You can find these negative thoughts and replace them with more positive ones, such as "I may not be perfect yet, but with practice and patience, I can get better and become a skilled guitar player": "*I can do all this through him who gives me strength*" (Philippians 4:13). This kind of positive self-talk can help you stay on track and motivated, which will make it easier to get through problems and setbacks.

We can learn new things and reach our goals by weeding our brains, but it can also make us feel better in general. We can live happier, more satisfying lives by getting rid of negative thoughts and replacing them with positive ones. This will help us feel less anxious, depressed, and stressed: "*Peace I leave with you; my peace I give you*" (John 14:27).

Brain weeding is like cleaning your mind and getting rid of all the things that are in the way. It helps us relax and feel less stressed. It can be very stressful to have too many things on our minds. But we'll feel better and more at ease once we get rid of all the junk: "*Cast all your anxiety on him because he cares for you*" (1 Peter 5:7).

You can get more done and focus better if you get rid of everything that isn't important. We can be more creative when we are calm, clear-headed, and focused. This is because there isn't much room for new ideas to come up when our minds are full of junk. Our brains will have more room to come up with great new ideas if we get rid of all the extra noise: "*Be still, and know that I am God*" (Psalm 46:10).

A good choice can show you how happy you will be. When our brains are all mixed up, it's hard to make good choices. But once we get rid of all the extra stuff, we can make better choices and live better lives.

Brain weeding can help you remember things better, not just when you need to make a choice. We all know that having too much information in our heads makes it harder to remember important things, like when we take tests. But if you throw away all the junk, you'll have more room in your brain to remember the things that matter.

We filter our thoughts so that bad or unclear ones are pushed out and good or helpful ones stay inside: "*Above all else, guard your heart, for everything you do flows from it*" (Proverbs 4:23).

You should also pay attention to what you read, watch, and listen to. Reading things we don't choose can make our minds messy.

Don't dwell on the past; only read things that are important and useful to you. When you think about the past, you can fill your head with thoughts and feelings that aren't helpful.

Let go of your anger, regrets, and grudges so you can think about the present and the future more: "*Forget the former things; do not dwell on the past. See, I am doing a new thing*!" (Isaiah 43:18-19).

Our minds are often full of nagging worries, intrusive thoughts, and bad mental habits that make it hard to think clearly and be creative in today's fast-paced world.

Brain weeding like gardening in that you look for and get rid of bad or useless thoughts on purpose. This gives you space to grow, focus, and be emotionally strong. You have to do it every day, like taking care of a garden to keep weeds from taking over.

Think of your brain as a piece of land that is full of life. Positive thoughts are like plants that give you food and fruit—ideas that make you feel good, push you to do better, and help you reach your goals.

Weeds are things that get in the way, like self-doubt ("I'm not good enough"), rumination ("Why did that meeting go wrong?"), or distractions ("I should check my phone again"). If you don't pull these weeds, they'll spread and take up space in your mind, blocking out the good stuff.

Getting rid of thoughts isn't about pushing them away; that just makes them stronger. It's about watching, accepting, and gently taking away instead. Cognitive behavioural therapy (CBT) research backs this up: regularly challenging negative patterns rewires neural pathways, just like trimming a plant makes its branches healthier.

The way your feet move in a rhythmic way while you walk creates a meditative flow that makes it easier to pull these mental weeds without judging them.

Step 1: Before you go for a walk, set an intention. Set a goal first. Take a moment to think about what you want to get done during your brain weeding session before you go outside. You might say to yourself, "Today, as I walk, I'll find three weeds and plant seeds of happiness in their place." Wear shoes that are comfortable and bring some water. If you can, keep your phone off or at home. Distractions are like weed killer.

Choose a route that you know well but that will keep you interested, like a loop through your neighbourhood, a trail in a park, or even city sidewalks with different sights and sounds.

Being consistent is the most important thing. Do it for 20 to 30 minutes every day if you can. When you start to walk, pay attention to how you breathe. Breathe in for four steps and then out for four. This helps you stay in the present and gives you room in your mind to watch your thoughts without getting stuck in them.

Step 2: Look for Weeds—Pay Attention. As you walk, let your mind wander, but stay alert like a gardener watching over their plot. You don't have to try to make thoughts happen; they will come to you. You should notice them, but not react right away. To find weeds, ask yourself these questions:

What am I thinking? If you keep worrying about work, money, or relationships, write it down as a weed. If you find yourself saying, "I'll never finish that project on time," stop and tell yourself, "That's a weed based on fear."

Is this idea good or bad? Weeds stop you from moving forward, but good thoughts help you move forward. A bad thought might be "Everything always goes wrong for me," while a good thought might be "What small step can I take next?"

How does my body feel? Weeds can show up in your body, like when you're stressed and your shoulders are tight or when you're worried and your stomach is knotted. When you have a bad thought while you're walking, pay attention to how your stride changes.

Practice this scanning for the first 5 to 10 minutes. If it's really overgrown (like after a long day), you might see groups of weeds that are related in your mind. For instance, you might see a chain of self-criticism that started with one thing.

Step 3: Get rid of the weeds—ways to get rid of them quickly. Once you've found it, it's time to pull. Don't pull them hard; instead, use gentle, evidence-based methods to get their roots to loosen:

Reframing: Use facts to fight the weed. Say it again in your head or out loud as you walk. Instead of saying "I'm terrible at public speaking," say "I've gotten better with practice, and one bad presentation doesn't define me."

You can see things in a new way when you get some fresh air and change your surroundings. For instance, seeing a strong tree bend in the wind might make you think of how flexible you are.

Gratitude's Replacement: After you pull up a plant, put in a new one. For every weed you pull, plant a seed of thanks. If you're feeling jealous

("Why does everyone else seem happier?"), say, "I'm grateful for my health and the peace and beauty of this path."

Gratitude walks can make you feel better by shifting your focus from what you don't have to what you do have.

Visualization: Imagine yourself pulling the weed out of the ground. As you move forward, imagine throwing the bad thought behind you and letting it sink into the ground. Do something physical, like shaking your hands or taking a deep breath, to make the release stronger.

If a weed is being stubborn because of things that happened in the past, write it down for later journaling or therapy. Don't let it stop you from walking. The goal is to get better, not to be perfect.

Step 4: Take care of the garden so that it grows well. You can't just pull weeds; you also need to add nutrients to the soil. Think about good things during the last half of your walk:

Affirmations in Motion: As you walk, say nice things. When you breathe in, say "I can," and when you breathe out, say "I let go of doubt." This gives you more energy and makes your walk like a moving meditation.

Sensory Engagement: Get rid of weeds with your senses. Hear the sound of leaves crunching underfoot, smell the fresh rain, or see how light plays on buildings. This keeps you in the here and now and stops new weeds from sprouting.

Seeds for Setting Goals: Make a list of what you want to do today. "I'm going to be interested in problems today." It's easier to remember them if you connect them to the endorphin rush you get from walking. If your mind starts to wander, gently bring your focus back to your breath or count your steps. It's normal; gardens don't get clean all at once.

Bad weather or not enough time? Change things up by walking around the house or having shorter sessions. Length doesn't matter as much as consistency.

Some weeds make you feel very strongly. If you think you can't handle pulling one, get help from a professional, like CBT sessions.

Adding brain weeding to your daily walk can help you feel less anxious, be more creative, focus better, and control your emotions better. Over time, your mental garden will be able to take care of itself, and fewer weeds will get in.

Remember that brain weeding is a skill that gets better the more you do it. Start small and be patient. Watch your mind get bigger. Put on your shoes, open the door, and start taking care of your inner garden right now. You will find your clearer, more colourful self at the end of the path.

RECONDITIONING

the MIND

I used to wake up every morning with my heart pounding like a drum in my chest, the same old fears already shouting before my eyes were fully open: you're not safe, you're too broken, you'll never be free again.

Trauma had moved into my mind and taken the master bedroom—years of betrayal, workplace wounds that cut deeper than I could name, the slow crumbling of a marriage I thought would last forever, and the quiet grief of losses that piled up until I could barely breathe.

My thoughts ruled me like a cruel king. But one ordinary Tuesday, with tears soaking my pillow, I opened my Bible and read these words that felt like cool water on burning skin: "***Do not be anxious about anything, but in every situation, by prayer and petition, with thanksgiving, present your requests to God. And the peace of God,*** *which transcends all understanding, will guard your hearts and your minds in Christ Jesus*" (Philippians 4:6–7).

In that moment I whispered, "Lord, I can't fix this mind on my own. Will You recondition it for me?" And that trembling yes became the first brick in a brand-new foundation.

The journey was slow and tender. I learned to bring every frightening thought straight to Him instead of wrestling alone. When the roar of a city bus made my body flood with panic, when a stranger's voice sounded too much like the man who once shattered my trust, when the sight of the area code 416 on a screen sent me spiraling, I would stop, breathe, and pray David's prayer: "*When I am afraid, I put my trust in You*" (Psalm 56:3). At first it felt like shouting into the wind, but little by little His peace really did stand guard over my heart the way He promised.

I wish I could tell you the change was instant, but there were whole seasons when the old thoughts roared back louder than ever. I remember the day I bravely went to the farmers' market with Kathleen—heart racing—just wanting to buy some vegetables and fruits like a normal person.

A group of ladies walked past, laughing, and one of them had the same build, the same tilt of the head as the supervisor who once broke me. My body decided we were in danger. I left the apples I was about to pick up, and asked Kathleen to keep walking with my head down. I cam home and cried in the shower.

Shame whispered, "See? You'll never be normal again." That night I opened my Bible to Psalm 147:3—"*He heals the brokenhearted and binds up their wounds*"—and I prayed through sobs, "Lord, bind this one too, please."

The next morning His mercies were new again (Lamentations 3:22–23), and I tried once more. One small trip became two. Two became staying long enough to smell the bread. Healing, I learned, is not a straight line; it is a faithful circle of returning to the One who never tires of welcoming us home.

There was another stretch of months when depression settled over me like a heavy, gray blanket. I lost my job, my energy, my desire to even get out of bed. Sleep was broken, appetite gone, hope thinner than paper.

On those days I clung to Isaiah 26:3 like a life raft: "*You will keep in perfect peace those whose minds are steadfast, because they trust in You.*"

My mind was anything but steadfast, but I began the gentlest practice of staying it on Him—three conscious breaths, one simple truth spoken aloud: "You are good. You are here. You love me."

Some mornings that was all I had. But three breaths became five minutes of quiet. Five minutes became a walk around the block. And one day, without warning, I laughed at something small and the sound startled me because it had been so long since joy visited. The Lord really does restore the years the locusts have eaten (Joel 2:25).

I surrounded myself with voices that echoed His. I chose friends who spoke life, books drenched in grace, music that sang of redemption. Proverbs 13:20 became my quiet prayer: "*Walk with the wise and become wise.*"

When negative people or places tried to pull me backward, I learned the gentle art of boundaries, remembering that even Jesus often withdrew to lonely places to pray (Luke 5:16).

I started writing three things I was grateful for every night—coffee, warm socks, the way the sky turns pink at dusk—and gratitude truly did become a shield against despair, just as 1 Thessalonians 5:18 promised.

Morning affirmations felt awkward at first, but I spoke them anyway because God's Word says we are transformed by the renewing of our minds (Romans 12:2).

In front of the mirror I would say, *"I am a new creation—the old has gone, the new has come"* (2 Corinthians 5:17). *"The Lord is my light and my salvation—whom shall I fear?"* (Psalm 27:1). *"I am fearfully and wonderfully made"* (Psalm 139:14). At first my voice shook, but over time the truth sank deeper than the lies ever had.

Therapy became sacred ground where the Holy Spirit and human kindness worked together. In the safety of that room I learned to name the trauma out loud, the betrayal, to let tears fall without shame, to watch God rewire the terror pathways in my brain while His Word washed the wounds.

Cognitive work, mindfulness, EMDR—all of it felt like the gentle hands of the Potter reshaping the clay (Jeremiah 18:6). And every time a memory lost its sting, I heard the quiet whisper of Isaiah 61:3: beauty for ashes, the oil of joy for mourning.

Today my mind is still a house under loving renovation. Some rooms are bright and finished; others still have scaffolding. But the difference is this: Jesus has the keys now. The old fears still knock sometimes, but they no longer own the place. When they come, I open the door and say with David, *"The Lord is my light and my salvation— whom shall I fear?"* And then I invite Jesus to sit with me in that room until it fills with light again.

The same God who calmed the storm on Galilee is calming the storm in you, whispering, *"Peace, be still"* (Mark 4:39). You are not stuck. You are being renewed, one surrendered thought, one faithful promise, one gentle morning at a time. And His Word will never return empty (Isaiah 55:11). It is alive, and it is reconditioning you right now into the likeness of Christ, whose mind you already carry (1 Corinthians 2:16). Keep going, beloved. The best rooms are still ahead.

Some years ago, I woke up every morning already defeated. My nervous system believed the betrayal was still happening, right now, in the present tense. My brain had done exactly what God designed it to do: it had learned perfectly how to keep me alive in a season that was no longer my reality. The problem was that the learning had become a prison.

Then I discovered two truths speaking the same language—one from the laboratory and one from the throne room of heaven—and they changed everything.

The laboratory truth is called neuroplasticity. Scientists used to believe that after childhood the brain was basically finished, like concrete that had set. We now know the opposite is true. Your brain is more like living clay. Every thought you think, every word you repeat, every memory you revisit sends tiny electrical impulses racing along neural pathways, and wherever those impulses travel most often, the brain lays down more myelin, more connections, stronger wires. In plain words: what you practice grows stronger.

The pathways that kept me frozen in fear had become eight-lane superhighways, built and reinforced by years of retraumatization. But the same brain that built those highways is also able to grow brand-new roads—quiet country lanes at first, then wider streets, then boulevards of peace—if I will simply begin traveling them on purpose. The technical names are long-term potentiation in the prefrontal cortex and long-term depression in the amygdala, but the everyday translation is gentler: new learning can quiet old fear.

The throne-room truth had been waiting for me all along in Romans 12:2: *"**Do not be conformed to this world, but be transformed by the renewing of your mind**."*

The Greek word for renewing, anakainosis, means a complete renovation, a making-new from the inside out. Before anyone had ever seen a living neuron, God told us that our minds are not fixed; they are designed to be renovated daily by His truth and His presence.

When I first put these two truths together, something in me exhaled for the first time in years.

Every morning I began a tiny act of cooperation with both the science and the Spirit. I would sit on the edge of my bed, place my hand over my racing heart, and speak Philippians 4:6–7 out loud: "*Father, I'm anxious again, but I'm bringing this to You with thanksgiving because You are good and You are here.*"

Then I would breathe slowly while picturing Jesus standing between me and the old memory. Nothing dramatic—just one minute of deliberate attention on Him instead of on the fear.

Neuroscientists would say I was interrupting the old circuit and firing a new one. The Bible would say I was taking every thought captive to the obedience of Christ (2 Corinthians 10:5).

Both would be right. In that minute, proteins like BDNF—brain-derived neurotrophic factor, the brain's own fertilizer—were being released, helping baby neurons sprout along the new pathway that said, "I am with Jesus, and I am safe."

Over weeks and months those baby neurons grew branches and myelin until the new pathway became strong and the old superhighway of terror began to crack and narrow.

Isaiah 26:3 became my daily promise and my daily practice: "**You will keep in perfect peace the mind that is stayed on You.**" I once heard that neuroimaging show that focused attention combined with trust actually increases gamma-wave synchrony between the thinking brain and the feeling brain. I have not done research on this, but it is believed to be true.

In other words, staying my mind on Jesus literally reorganizes the electrical activity of my brain toward peace. God knew this long before we had the machines to measure it.

On the hardest days, when shame tried to tell me I was permanently damaged, I answered with 2 Corinthians 5:17 spoken out loud: "**If anyone is in Christ, the new creation has come. The old has gone, the new is here.**"

Each repetition was a tiny vote for the new pathway. Each time I chose to speak life instead of death, the synapse that carried life grew a little stronger, and the synapse that carried shame grew a little weaker. He heals the brokenhearted and binds up their wounds (Psalm 147:3), and sometimes the binding happens one strengthened connection at a time.

I learned that gratitude is neurological medicine. Writing three things I was thankful for every night—warm water, the sound of rain, the stubborn beat of my own heart—released dopamine and serotonin, chemicals that make it easier for the brain to form new positive memories. First Thessalonians 5:18 is not just a command; it is a prescription written by the Great Physician who wired the brain.

Even lament is part of the rewiring. When the grief felt too heavy, I poured it out exactly as the psalmists did, and discovered that honest crying in His presence lowers cortisol and activates the parasympathetic nervous system. The brain learns, *"I can feel everything and still be held."*

Today, the old pathway still flickers for half a second when triggered—old habits die hard—but the new pathway is now the main road. Peace arrives faster than panic. Joy is no longer a stranger. My brain has been literally reshaped by the truth I chose to practice and the Presence I chose to stay in.

You and I serve a God who built neuroplasticity into every neuron because He always planned to make all things new—not just in heaven someday, but in our actual synapses right now. He is the Potter and we are the clay (Jeremiah 18:6), and every time we return to His Word, His presence, and His love, He is gently, faithfully, scientifically reshaping us from the inside out.

Your brain is not your enemy and it is not your prison. It is God's living workshop, and the Master Craftsman is already at work. All He asks is that we keep bringing Him the raw material—one thought, one breath, one verse, one surrendered moment at a time—until the day we discover, to our wondering delight, that we have quietly, steadily, miraculously received the mind of Christ (1 Corinthians 2:16).

REGROUPING

the

I used to believe that a scattered mind was simply my new normal, that after everything I had walked through the chaos would always be louder than the calm. The trauma and betrayal had left fragments everywhere: one minute I was functioning, sending emails and smiling at the grocery clerk, the next minute a sound or a smell or a date on the calendar would hurl me back into the old terror and every thought would scatter like startled birds.

I lived waiting for the next crash. Then one ordinary Thursday, sitting on my bedroom floor surrounded by torn pieces of paper on which I had scribbled every fear that was screaming at once, I opened the Bible and read the story of the disciples in the boat.

A furious storm had come up on the lake, waves were breaking over the boat, it was nearly swamped, and Jesus was asleep on a cushion. The disciples woke him in panic: *"Teacher, don't you care if we drown?"* He got up, rebuked the wind and said to the waves, *"Quiet! Be still!"* Then the wind died down and it was completely calm. He turned to them and asked, *"Why are you so afraid? Do you still have no faith?"* (Mark 4:35–40).

Jesus was not concerned about the storm as He has an asisgnment waiting for him. Jesus was not afraid of the storm. He was not worried at all. Do you know why? Because He had important work waiting on the other side of the lake.

On the other side, in a place called Gerasene, there was a man who needed help. This man was naked. He lived among the tombs. Many demons were inside him. The demons made him strong and wild. People tried to put chains on him, but he broke every chain. He cried and hurt himself day and night.

Jesus came across the lake for that one man. The storm tried to stop Him, but it could not. Jesus wanted to make the man free and happy again. That is why He slept peacefully in the boat. He knew God's love was stronger than any storm.

In that moment I understood something new: the storm outside the boat is one thing, but the real danger is the storm inside the boat—the storm in the mind. And Jesus has authority over both. He still speaks *"Peace, be still"* to the wind and the waves, and he still speaks it to the frantic thoughts that threaten to swamp us.

That day on the floor became the first time I deliberately practiced regrouping. I did not try to argue with every fear. I simply gathered the torn pieces of paper, laid them in a pile, placed my hand on them and said, "Lord, these are the waves breaking over my boat right now. You are in the boat with me. Speak peace." I waited. Nothing dramatic happened—no lightning, no sudden rush of emotion—but after a few minutes the roar inside quieted to a whisper.

I was able to stand up, make coffee, and go on with the day. It was not the last storm, but it was the first time I discovered that Jesus sleeps in my boat on purpose, because he is never actually asleep to my cries.

A few months later I faced a different kind of scattering: the kind that comes from too many open doors and too many good things pulling at me.

I had said yes to speaking engagements, writing deadlines, family needs, ministry opportunities, and suddenly every hour was accounted for and my mind was a jumbled calendar of guilt and dread. I felt like the Israelites at the Red Sea—Pharaoh's army behind me, deep water in front, and no visible way through.

One night I could not sleep, so I got up and read Exodus 14. The people were terrified and crying out, *"Was it because there were no graves in Egypt that you brought us to the desert to die?"* Moses answered, *"Do not be afraid. Stand firm and you will see the deliverance the Lord will bring you today… The Lord will fight for you; you need only to be still."*

The Hebrew is the same "rapha" again—let your hands fall, stop striving, release your grip. So I did something that felt ridiculous: I took my paper calendar, laid it on the kitchen table, and physically opened my hands over it, palms down, then palms up in surrender. I whispered, "Lord, You fight for me. I am being still."

The next morning two engagements cancelled themselves, one deadline was extended, and a friend offered practical help I had been too proud to ask for. The sea did not part, but a way opened where there had seemed to be no way. Regrouping had made room for the miracle.

There was also the long season of anger that threatened to scatter me completely. I had been betrayed by people I trusted in the workplace, of all places, and the wound felt like David's when he wrote Psalm 55: *"If an enemy were insulting me, I could endure it… But it is you, a man like myself, my companion, my close friend."* Nights I lay awake rehearsing what I wished I had said, imagining confrontations that would leave them speechless, nursing the acid of resentment until it burned holes in my stomach.

One Sunday the pastor read Ephesians 4:26–27—*"In your anger do not sin: Do not let the sun go down while you are still angry, and do not give the devil a foothold"*—and I felt the Holy Spirit nudge me gently: *"How many suns have gone down on this anger?"* Hundreds.

That night I dragged myself out of bed at two in the morning, opened my journal, and wrote the ugliest, most honest letter I have ever written. Every accusation, every hurt, every tear. Then at the bottom I wrote, "Jesus, I give this anger to You. I choose forgiveness because You forgave me when I was Your enemy." I signed it, dated it, and burned it in the fireplace.

The next morning I woke lighter than I had in years. The people had not changed, but my mind had been regrouped around the cross instead of the wound. David knew this path too—he poured out his complaint before the Lord in the psalms, then always ended with *"But I trust in your unfailing love"* (Psalm 13). Regrouping is learning to pour out the poison and then drink from the fountain of His love.

Grief brought another scattering. After my friend's marriage ended and several close relationships dissolved in the same season, I felt like a tree stripped bare in winter. My thoughts circled endlessly around what had been lost, what would never be again, what could I have done to help my friends. And within a few years later we had five couples close to us seperated. It was difficult to support them individually without being looked upon as we favoured one over the other. It brought grief knowing I support many couple's in couple's therapy but could not support my own friends.

The grief did not disappear, but it stopped owning the center of my mind. Like Job, who said, *"Though he slay me, yet will I hope in him"* (Job 13:15), I learned to regroup my thoughts around hope instead of despair.

Even physical illness forced me into regrouping I would never have chosen. There were months when chronic back pain and fatigue made every day feel like climbing a mountain with a broken leg. My mind kept screaming, "This will never end. God has forgotten you. You are useless now."

One morning I could barely get out of bed, so I stayed there and slowly recited the only verses I could remember through the fog: Psalm 23. "*The Lord is my shepherd, I lack nothing. He makes me lie down in green pastures…*"

I realised He was making me lie down. The illness was like the shepherd's rod and staff forcing me to rest when I would not rest myself. I began to regroup my thoughts around His nearness instead of my pain. 2 Corinthians 12:9 became my daily bread: "*My grace is sufficient for you, for my power is made perfect in weakness.*"

I stopped fighting the lying-down and started receiving it as love. The pain did not vanish, but the terror did. My mind learned a new default setting: weakness is the place where His strength shows up best.

There was the terrifying season of decision paralysis, when too many good doors stood open and I was afraid of choosing the wrong one. I felt like the rich young ruler who walked away sad because he had great wealth and could not let go. My mind spun in circles: "If I choose this, I'll miss that. If I say no here, I'll disappoint them. What if I ruin everything?"

I remembered Joshua standing before the Jordan in flood stage, the people trembling, and God's strange instruction: "*Consecrate yourselves, for tomorrow the Lord will do amazing things among you*" (Joshua 3:5).

So I consecrated a whole day—no phone, no input, just silence, worship, and walking. I asked one question: "Lord, what is the next obedient step?" Not ten steps, one.

The answer came quietly while I walked beside the river at Dick's dam: "Write the book you keep saying you don't have time for." That was six years ago. Every page you are reading now is evidence that regrouping makes room for miracles.

Regrouping was simply turning toward home.

These stories are not exceptions; they are the pattern. Gideon hiding in the winepress, convinced he was the least of the least, until an angel called him mighty warrior and he began to think, speak, and act from that new identity.

Elijah under the broom tree asking God to let him die, until God fed him, let him sleep, and then whispered truth in the gentle breeze.

Peter sinking in the water crying "Lord, save me!" and Jesus immediately reaching out his hand.

Every one of them experienced a moment when their thoughts were scattered by fear, shame, or despair, and every one of them learned—slowly, imperfectly—to regroup those thoughts around the presence and promise of God.

That is still the invitation today. When your mind feels like a storm-tossed boat, a house with every light blazing and every door banging in the wind, remember that the One who quieted Galilee is in your boat. He is not alarmed by the mess. He is not impatient with your scattered pieces. He is simply waiting for you to lift your eyes, open your hands, and say, "Lord, here is the chaos. Speak peace."

And He will. Sometimes in a whisper, sometimes in a Scripture that suddenly burns in your heart, sometimes in the quiet after you have poured out every tear like Hannah. He will gather what is scattered, separate light from darkness, and set your feet on solid ground again.

I still practice regrouping every single day, because the house still gets messy. Some mornings it is five minutes with a cup of coffee and

Psalm 143:8: *"Let the morning bring me word of your unfailing love, for I have put my trust in you."*

Some evenings it is half an hour in the back yard by the fire pit, or in my garden naming everything that felt heavy and laying it at the cross. Some nights it is simply falling asleep whispering "Jesus" until the name itself becomes the regrouping.

The scattered pieces are no longer evidence that something is wrong with me. They are evidence that I am alive in a broken world, and that I belong to a Saviour who specialises in gathering, restoring, and making beautiful things out of chaos.

The same Spirit who hovered over the formless void at creation hovers over the formless voids in us, waiting for our surrendered "Let there be light."

Brain regrouping is not the same as reconditioning or restructuring, though it walks hand in hand with both. Reconditioning is the long, slow renovation – rewiring the very pathways. Restructuring is replacing one lie with one truth, one thought at a time. Regrouping is what you do in the middle of the storm when everything is flying: you stop, gently and deliberately, gather the scattered pieces, lay them on the table before the Lord, and ask Him to show you what belongs, what must be released, and what order He wants to bring. It is the spiritual discipline of bringing order out of chaos, one surrendered breath at a time.

The Bible begins with regrouping. Genesis 1:2 tells us the earth was formless and empty, darkness was over the surface of the deep – *tohu va-vohu* in Hebrew, a chaotic jumble – and the Spirit of God was hovering over the waters. Then God spoke, and light came. Then He separated. Then He gathered. Then named. Every creative act was a regrouping: gathering the scattered, ordering the disordered, bringing beauty out of confusion. That is what He still does in our minds when we let Him.

There was a season when my mind felt exactly like that formless void. After the workplace betrayal, the financial strain – everything hit at once. I woke every morning to a mental blizzard.

One moment I was reliving the supervisor's voice, the next I was terrified of not knowing my future, then convinced I was dying of some undiagnosed disease, then drowning in shame for still being broken after a few months.

My thoughts were not just negative; they were fragmented, overlapping, screaming. I could not finish a sentence without three other sentences crashing into it. I remember sitting in my car in the grocery store parking lot, hands gripping the wheel, unable to go inside because the thought-avalanche had started again and I could not stop it.

That was the day I first practiced true regrouping.

I did not try to fix everything. I did not even try to challenge every thought. I simply closed my eyes and prayed the shortest prayer I knew: "Lord Jesus Christ, have mercy on me."

Over and over, like the Jesus Prayer of the desert fathers. And slowly, the storm quieted enough for me to take one step: I opened my journal and wrote at the top of the page, "What is true right now?"

Then I wrote what I knew: I am sitting in my car. It is Tuesday. The sun is shining. Jesus is with me. I wrote four lines, no more. Then I wrote, "What can I do in the next five minutes?" Answer: breathe, start the car, drive home if I need to, or walk into the store one aisle at a time. I chose one aisle. I bought icecream. I came home. And something in me exhaled.

That was regrouping: gathering the chaos, laying it before Him, letting Him separate light from darkness in me.

Psalm 46:10 became the verse that carried me through that season: ***Be still, and know that I am God.***" The Hebrew word for "be still" is rapha – let go, release, sink down, relax your grip. It is the same word used when God tells the Israelites to stop striving against the Egyptians at the Red Sea and watch Him fight for them (Exodus 14:14).

Regrouping is learning to rapha – to release the frantic grip on every flying thought and let the Lord separate the waters.

Another morning, months later, I woke up to a different kind of chaos: the busy kind. Deadlines stacked like Jenga blocks, children needing things, messages piling up, a speaking engagement I had said yes to in Germany and France when I was feeling brave and now felt impossible.

My mind was a browser with seventy tabs open, all playing music at once. I could feel the old familiar tightness in my chest – the one that used to precede panic attacks. This time I caught it early. I went to the kitchen, put the kettle on, and did the thing that has now become ritual: I took a blank page and drew a simple cross in the middle. On the left arm I wrote everything I was carrying that was not mine to carry that day – other people's expectations, hypothetical disasters, shame from yesterday. On the right arm I wrote what was mine to do today – three things, no more.

At the top I wrote Isaiah 30:15: "***In returning and rest you shall be saved; in quietness and trust shall be your strength***." Then I prayed over each item on the left, "Lord, I give this to You," and over each item on the right, "Lord, multiply my time and strength."

I left the page on the counter all day. Every time I passed it, I touched the cross and breathed. That day was one of the most productive and peaceful I can remember.

That is regrouping: returning, resting, quieting, trusting.

There was the season of anger. I had been wronged – deeply, repeatedly, unfairly. Nights I lay awake rehearsing conversations I wished I had had with Kathleen, words I wished I could unsay, revenge fantasies I hated myself for entertaining. My thoughts were a furnace.

One night the Holy Spirit brought Ephesians 4:26-27 to mind: *"**Be angry and do not sin; do not let the sun go down on your anger, and give no opportunity to the devil.**"*

I realised the sun had gone down on my anger many times. So I got out of bed at 2 a.m., opened my journal, and wrote the anger a letter – every ugly, honest word. Then I wrote Jesus' name at the bottom and signed it "Forgiven by the blood of the Lamb."

I tore the pages into tiny pieces and flushed them. Then I wrote a new page: every blessing the painful situation had produced – growth, empathy, deeper prayer life, new boundaries. I read Psalm 103 aloud: *"**Bless the Lord, O my soul, and forget not all his benefits.**"* By the time I finished, the furnace had cooled to embers, and I slept. The next morning I woke up lighter.

That is regrouping: naming the fire, offering it to Jesus, letting Him replace bitterness with blessing.

There was the season of grief when our second daughter had a miscarriage after being five months pregnant. Loss left me feeling like a tree stripped bare in winter. My mind kept returning to what was gone, what would never be again.

One afternoon I sat on the floor with my Bible open to Job, feeling sorry for myself, my daughter and our family. I knew that Job got his stuff back in the end but I was not sure I would be a grandfather.

The Lord whispered, "Read the middle, not the end." So I read Job 23:10: *"**When he has tried me, I shall come out as gold.**"* Then Job 42:5: *"**I had heard of you by the hearing of the ear, but now my eye sees you.**"*

I realised the point was not restoration of things but intimacy with Him. I took a walk that day and began a new practice: every time a grief-thought came, I finished it with "but now my eye sees You."

The loss is real, but now my eye sees You. The dream died, but now my eye sees You. I still cry sometimes, but the grief has been regrouped around His face instead of my pain.

That is regrouping: bringing the stripped branches to the Gardener and letting Him decide what spring looks like.

When my thoughts are loudest, my body often needs to move. A walk, a run, even pacing the living room while praying in tongues – motion helps the scattered pieces settle.

Science says bilateral stimulation (walking, dancing) helps process trauma. Scripture says David danced before the Lord with all his might (2 Samuel 6:14). I think both are right.

There were days the thoughts are too heavy to regroup alone. I text a friend: "Pray for me – mind is loud." Or I call my pastor and simply say, "Can we have lunch?" Proverbs 11:14 is true: in an abundance of counselors there is safety. Sometimes the most spiritual thing I can do is let someone else help me gather the pieces.

The Scripture itself is the ultimate regrouping tool. I have selected scriptures when fear of abandonment rises, Deuteronomy 31:8: *"He will never leave you nor forsake you."* When guilt attacks, Romans 8:1: *"There is therefore now no condemnation for those who are in Christ Jesus."* When I feel orphaned, Psalm 27:10: *"Though my father and mother forsake me, the Lord will receive me."*

I read them aloud. I sing them. I write them on my journal. The Word enters my ears, my eyes, my voice, my body, and slowly orders the chaos from the inside.

Regrouping is not a one-time event; it is a rhythm. Some days it takes two minutes, some days two hours. Some seasons it is daily, some seasons hourly. But every single time I practice it, I am changed a little more into the likeness of the One who spoke order into chaos and still speaks it into me.

I used to think peace was the absence of storms. Now I know peace is the presence of the Prince of Peace in the middle of them, gathering my scattered thoughts like a shepherd gathering lambs, carrying them close to His heart (Isaiah 40:11).

If your mind feels like a ransacked house today, hear this: the Owner has not abandoned the property. He is walking through every room with you, picking up the broken pieces, speaking light into the darkness, saying, "Let there be order here." All He asks is that you pause, open the door, and let Him in.

One thought at a time.

One breath at a time.

One verse at a time.

He is faithful to complete the good work He began (Philippians 1:6), and the beautiful, lifelong work of regrouping your mind until the day you see Him face to face and every scattered piece falls into perfect, eternal place.

Until then, keep gathering. Keep surrendering. Keep trusting.

The house is becoming a home again. And the Master of the house is already inside, singing over you with love.

MAINTAINING
the

I was thirty-two when my mind began to betray me. I was preaching on Sunday, teaching at the Bible College, working at a group home with ABI clients, doing midweek Bible study, studying my master's degree, and trying to be the husband and father my wife and four daughters deserved. I told myself the fatigue was normal. I bragged that I could get by on five hours of sleep the way other men brag about bench-pressing three plates. I quoted 2 Corinthians 12:9—"***My grace is sufficient for you, for my power is made perfect in weakness***"—while ignoring the fact that Paul wrote those words after God refused to remove a genuine affliction, not a self-inflicted wound.

Then came the Sunday I lost the book of Haggai.

I was in the pulpit, mid-sentence, referencing the prophet who told Zerubbabel that the glory of the latter house would be greater than the former. I reached for the chapter and verse the way I had a thousand times before and found nothing. The reference was simply gone. My mind was a blank wall. I stood there for what felt like an hour but was probably four seconds, sweat beading under the lights, while the people waited. I finally said, "It's in the minor prophets somewhere," and moved on. The congregation laughed kindly. I wanted to disappear.

That night I sat in my van in the dark parking lot and did something I had not done since I was a boy: I cried. Not polite pastoral tears, but the ugly, choking kind. I was terrified. I had always been the sharpest guy in the room—remembered every name, every verse, every job-site measurement. Now I was forgetting why I walked into Home Depot, could not recall how I got to point B from point A, could not find my keys as I forgot leaving them in the refrigerator, and staring at my open Bible unable to string two thoughts together. I whispered into the steering wheel, "Lord, if You take my mind, You take everything."

He did not speak audibly, but over the next two years He rebuilt my brain the way He once rebuilt the walls of Jerusalem—one ordinary stone at a time, with plenty of opposition, mockery, and sweat. What I learned was not a program, not a supplement regimen, not a productivity hack. It was stewardship. The brain is the only organ through which we love God with all our mind. To let it rust is not humility; it is ingratitude.

This is the record of how a stubborn man learned brain maintenance from the Book he thought he already knew by heart.

It began, humiliatingly, with sleep.

I had treated sleep the way some men treat tithe: whatever was left over after everything more "important" was done. I wore forty-five-hour days like a medal. I mocked men who needed eight hours as soft. Then I read Psalm 127:2 again, the verse I had quoted to anxious fathers while ignoring its rebuke to me: "*It is in vain that you rise up early and go late to rest, eating the bread of anxious toil; for he gives to his beloved sleep.*"

I looked up the Hebrew. The word for sleep is yeshen—deep, undisturbed, restorative. The same root appears in Genesis 2:21 when God caused a deep sleep to fall upon Adam before He built the woman from his rib. God does surgery while we sleep. He knits raveled nerves (Psalm 127 is quoting the same idea as Psalm 4:8—"*In peace I will both lie down and sleep; for you alone, O Lord, make me dwell in safety*"). While I was scrolling X at 1 a.m. arguing with strangers about predestination, the Lord was trying to take out my neurological trash and I kept locking the door.

I made a covenant. For ninety days I would be in bed by ten and up at six. No phone in the bedroom. No "just one more email." The first week I lay awake staring at the ceiling, convinced the kingdom would collapse without my vigilance. Nothing collapsed. The elders handled the emergency calls. My wife smiled more. My sermons actually got clearer because I wasn't stringing thoughts together on caffeine and pride.

By week six the fog began to lift. I remembered Haggai 2:9 without looking it up. I could feel individual synapses firing again like cold engines turning over after a long winter. I learned later that during slow-wave sleep the brain's glymphatic system opens and washes away beta-amyloid, tau proteins, alpha-synuclein—literally the garbage that clogs the mind and leads to dementia. God designed a nightly power-washing cycle, and I had been skipping it for a decade.

Sleep was the first brick.

The second was food.

I grew up on rice, roti, yams, cassava, three thousand calories a day swinging a hammer. I could put away a plate full of carbs and meat, and preach an hour later without missing a beat. I mocked vegetarians the way some men mock poetry. Then I hit 230 pounds, my triglycerides went over 400, and my wedding ring could not fit me. The doctor used the phrase "pre-diabetic" and I laughed.

I opened my Bible angry, demanding the Lord tell me why a man couldn't eat what he wants. Instead He took me to Daniel 1. Four young Hebrews in Babylonian captivity refused the king's rich food and wine and asked for pulse—beans, lentils, vegetables—and water. Ten days later they were fairer and fatter than all the youths who ate the king's delicacies. The Hebrew phrase means healthier and better nourished. I had always read that as a spiritual miracle. It was also a nutritional one.

I did my own test. We decided as a family to do the Daniel fast. No sweets, no meats, no caffeine, only fruits and vegetables. I felt like I was starving for three days. On day four I woke up without the usual brain fog. On day seven I ran five kilometers without planning to. On day ten I stepped on the scale and had lost eleven pounds, but more importantly I could think again. Words came when I called them. Sermon illustrations arrived unbidden. I felt like someone had turned the lights back on upstairs. We joined the gym as a family.

I kept going. I learned that the omega-3s in wild salmon cross the blood-brain barrier and reduce inflammation. That the polyphenols in blueberries increase BDNF—the fertilizer that grows new neurons. That the medium-chain triglycerides in coconut oil provide clean fuel when glucose is scarce. That fasting sixteen hours a day (the way the early church often did before feasts) triggers autophagy, cellular housekeeping. I was not chasing health food fads. I was rediscovering the diet of Eden, the diet of the wilderness, the diet of the kingdom that is coming—olives, fish, wine, bread, honey, pomegranates, lamb later on that year became my favourite foods.

Deuteronomy 8:3 hit me between the eyes: *"**Man lives by every word that comes from the mouth of the Lord.**"* Yes, ultimately the Word made flesh. But also the word that spoke walnuts into existence— shaped like brains, packed with DHA. The word that made the olive tree and the salmon and the bitter herbs of Passover. The same God who feeds us with living bread designed food that feeds living brains. I had been living on the king's rations and wondering why I felt captive.

The third brick was movement.

I had always been strong—worked as a drywall taper, then in group homes, with men in Federal parole. I was active skiing and running around with the children. But cardio? That was for runners, not real men. Then I read that Elijah outran Ahab's chariot from Carmel to Jezreel, a distance of nearly twenty miles after calling down fire and slaughtering 450 prophets. The man was fifty years old at least. I tried to imagine doing that after a days work preaching three services and felt convicted.

I started walking with Kathleen and the children, praying the Psalms out loud. Ten minutes became thirty. Thirty became an hour. Then one January morning I started running at the gym. I made it half a kilometer before I thought I would die. I kept at it. Six months later I would run eight to ten kilometers without stopping, weeping at eight because I could feel my brain singing.

Exercise, I learned, is the only thing proven to increase hippocampal volume in adults—the part that turns short-term memory into long-term, the part that shrinks under chronic stress. Every footfall releases BDNF, myostatin, irisn—miracle grow for the mind. Paul knew it when he told Timothy that bodily training is of some value. Some. Not all. But some. Enough to mention while chained in a Roman cell.

The fourth brick was the hardest: learning the sacred word "no."

I had said yes to every board (Pioneer Clubs Canada), every committee, every counselling appointment, every late-night phone call, every job opportunity. I thought availability was love. My cortisol stayed elevated so long my adrenal glands felt like raisins. Chronic high cortisol eats the hippocampus the way termites eat a foundation.

Jesus did not heal every sick person in Palestine. He withdrew when the crowds pressed. He slept in a storm while disciples panicked. He told Martha that only one thing was necessary and Mary had chosen it.

Isaiah 30:15 became a lifeline: ***"In returning and rest you shall be saved; in quietness and in trust shall be your strength."***

The fifth brick was brotherhood.

Proverbs 27:17—*"**Iron sharpens iron, and one man sharpens another.**"* I thought that meant debate club. It doesn't. It means friction in relationship. I had plenty of colleagues and church members and Facebook friends, but no man who could look me in the eye and say, "You're killing yourself and calling it ministry."

I asked friends to meet me once a month. No agenda except truth and dinner. We asked three questions: What is killing you? What is life-giving? Where are you tempted to lie? One of them told me if I didn't cancel two speaking engagements he would call the hosts himself and tell them I was sick. I cancelled. Another made me hand over my phone on Friday nights. They saved my mind the way Jonathan saved David's—by covenant love that refused to watch me self-destruct.

The sixth brick was awe.

I had reduced the faith to propositions and projects. Sunsets were just weather. My children's laughter was background noise. My brain's default mode network—the part that wanders and wonders and consolidates memory—was starving.

I started studying creation again the way I studied Greek in Bible College. I lay on the yard at night learning constellations because Psalm 19 says the heavens declare. I planted a garden and watched seeds die and rise. I read Job 38-41 every spring until I shut my mouth in wonder.

Neuroscience later confirmed that awe shrinks the ego and grows the cortex. The Bible said it first: *"**Be still and know that I am God.**"* Stillness is not empty. It is full of neurons rewiring around glory.

There were smaller bricks too. Laughter—Proverbs 17:22 is biology as much as poetry. Singing—melody engages both hemispheres; no wonder Ephesians 5 tells us to sing psalms. Fasting—ketones clear brain fog and heighten prayer the way they heightened Jesus' ministry after forty days. Even cold showers—turns out deliberate stress (hormesis) makes the brain resilient the way lifting tears muscle to make it stronger.

The real miracle was quieter. I enjoyed God again. I enjoyed my wife's laughter. I enjoyed watching my children grow into young adults. I enjoyed the mind He gave me—the terrible, wonderful responsibility of loving Him with all of it.

Last month I found the journal from the dark year. One entry read: "I think my mind is dying and I don't know how to stop it." I took it out to the fire pit and burned it page by page, watching the words curl into smoke. Then prayed the way one would pray when they have been to the edge and brought back.

Wherever you are, hear a man who lost his mind and got it back: the brain God gave you is not a machine to be red-lined until it blows. It is a garden entrusted to your care. The Gardener still walks there in the cool of the day, waiting to show you which weeds need pulling, which trees need pruning, which fountains need unblocking.

Start tonight with sleep. He gives to His beloved in their sleep.

Start tomorrow with food that honours the temple.

Start moving—walk with Him while you pray.

Start saying no—the yoke He measured fits your shoulders exactly.

Start laughing again—medicine for the bones and the synapses.

Start looking up—the heavens still declare.

And if you forget everything else, remember this: the mind you are tempted to treat as a tool is actually the holy ground where you meet the living God. Take off your shoes. Tend it well. He is jealous for every neuron because He is jealous for fellowship with you.

He who began a good work in you will be faithful to complete it—down to the last axon, the last dendrite, the last quiet thought in the middle of the night when you realize you are fearfully, wonderfully, unbreakably His.

I know. He did it for me.

RENEWING

the

Renewing our minds means regaining access to the mental potential with which we were born. It is reclaiming the sound mind, the peace, and the strength God has already blessed us with: *"**For God has not given us a spirit of fear, but of power and of love and of a sound mind**"* (2 Timothy 1:7).

Life's wilderness (anxiety, stress, failure, money problems, broken relationships) buried that gift, but Jesus came to set us free and restore what was lost. *"**The thief comes only to steal and kill and destroy; I have come that they may have life, and have it to the full**"* (John 10:10). Don't worry; we can get it back.

There will be ups and downs on this journey, but in the end the victory is already ours because *"**thanks be to God, who gives us the**" *victory through our Lord Jesus Chris*t" (1 Corinthians 15:57). So let's finish this glorious journey by renewing our minds together.

Our lives swing continually between sunny days and gloomy evenings. We often feel weighed down by the stresses and worries of daily living. Negative thoughts and emotions can cling to us and refuse to let go. When that heaviness settles in, it is a clear sign: it's time to renew your mind!

Renewing your mind is about stepping back, clearing out the mental clutter and negativity that hold you captive, and choosing to refresh your perspective with truth and hope. *"Do not conform to the pattern of this world, but be transformed by the renewing of your mind"* (Romans 12:2).

It takes effort and commitment, yet the reward is priceless, and it is far easier than you think because the Holy Spirit Himself is the One doing the heavy lifting. Ultimately, renewing our minds is the path to the abundant, joyful life Jesus promised: *"I came that they may have life, and have it abundantly"* (John 10:10 ESV).

Renewing the mind is not a single technique; it is an ongoing lifestyle built on many strategies that touch both our mental and physical selves. On the days when overwhelm, stress, and runaway thoughts attack, we need practices that do more than distract us—they must help us regain true control.

Mindfulness rooted in God's presence, meditation on Scripture, and deep breathing exercises can make a dramatic difference. By releasing unwanted thoughts and anchoring ourselves in the present moment with Jesus, we become centered and calm: *"You will keep in perfect peace those whose minds are steadfast, because they trust in you"* (Isaiah 26:3). Add journaling, and we gain clarity and direction: *"Write the vision; make it plain on tablets"* (Habakkuk 2:2).

A friend of our had lost her husband in a tragic car accident. Grief, anxiety, and PTSD crashed over her like waves. She was on the edge of giving up. Alongside counselling and medical care, we encouraged her to begin renewing her mind through daily gratitude.

Every evening she wrote three things she was still thankful for—some days it was simply "I breathed today," "the sun rose," or "my dog licked my face." Slowly, gratitude rewired her heart. *"Give thanks in all circumstances; for this is God's will for you in Christ Jesus"* (1 Thessalonians 5:18).

Over time she felt stronger, more hopeful, and the dark thoughts lost their grip. Today she leads a grief-support group and tells everyone, "Gratitude didn't erase my pain, but it gave me back my life." Whether we face grief, stress, anxiety, or simply feel stuck, renewing our minds is God's proven way to break free and step into the full life He planned for us.

There are countless techniques we can use, depending on what the Holy Spirit highlights for each of us. Some find meditation on Scripture and mindfulness in God's presence brings deep peace: *"Great peace have those who love your law, and nothing can make them stumble"* (Psalm 119:165).

Others discover that brain-dumping onto paper or journaling sorts their emotions and reveals truth. Many practice gratitude, set biblical intentions, or pursue activities that spark joy and fulfillment—anything from worship to gardening to serving others.

Sometimes the breakthrough is as simple as stepping away from social media and negativity and fixing our eyes on what is lovely: *"Finally, brothers and sisters, whatever is true, whatever is noble, whatever is right, whatever is pure, whatever is lovely, whatever is admirable—if anything is excellent or praiseworthy—think about such things"* (Philippians 4:8). Renewing your mind takes effort and commitment, but the fruit is eternal—and it is worth every moment.

Renewing our minds changes our thought patterns and perspectives, dramatically improving our mental and emotional well-being. It is the intentional replacement of negative, self-limiting beliefs with the truth of God's Word: *"We take captive every thought to make it obedient to Christ"* (2 Corinthians 10:5).

It is shifting our gaze from what is wrong to what is right, from what we lack to what He has already provided, from what we cannot do to what He can do through us: *"I can do all this through him who gives me strength"* (Philippians 4:13).

The benefits are life-changing. First, when we refuse to let our minds stagnate, we break cycles of negative thinking and step into the peace Jesus promised: *"Peace I leave with you; my peace I give you"* (John 14:27).

Second, renewing our minds births a growth mindset that sees every trial as training in the hands of a loving Father: *"Consider it pure joy, my brothers and sisters, whenever you face trials of many kinds, because you know that the testing of your faith produces perseverance"* (James 1:2-3).

Third, renewed minds produce better relationships because we become quick to listen, slow to speak, and slow to become angry (James 1:19), walking in love, empathy, and forgiveness.

Finally, it opens the door to continual growth and confidence: *"Forgetting what is behind and straining toward what is ahead, I press on toward the goal to win the prize for which God has called me heavenward in Christ Jesus"* (Philippians 3:13-14).

Science now confirms what Scripture declared long ago: renewing our minds literally reshapes our brains through neuroplasticity. When we replace lies with truth, practice gratitude, or meditate on God's Word, we strengthen pathways of peace and weaken pathways of fear.

Mindfulness and Scripture meditation thicken the prefrontal cortex (better decision-making) and calm the amygdala (less fear and anxiety). Exercise grows the hippocampus (sharper memory and learning).

Gratitude rewires us for joy. All of this echoes the promise: "***Be transformed by the renewing of your mind***" (Romans 12:2).

God designed our brains to be changed by beholding Him: "***And we all, who with unveiled faces contemplate the Lord's glory, are being transformed into his image with ever-increasing glory***" (2 Corinthians 3:18).

This is why transforming our thinking can heal disease, restore careers, rebuild marriages, break addictions, raise grades, and win lifelong friends. "***As he thinks in his heart, so is he***" (Proverbs 23:7 NKJV). Change the thought, and you change the life.

No matter how dark the valley feels right now, you have been given authority to renew your mind and step into freedom: "***The weapons we fight with are not the weapons of the world. On the contrary, they have divine power to demolish strongholds***" (2 Corinthians 10:4).

It is not easy, and it is not instant, but it is guaranteed because the Spirit who raised Jesus from the dead lives in you and is renewing your mind right now (Romans 8:11).

Here are a few more proven practices, each anchored in Scripture:

- Cognitive-Behavioural Therapy (CBT) rooted in truth: identifying and replacing lies the way Paul teaches in 2 Corinthians 10:5.
- Mindfulness Meditation on God's Word: "***I have hidden your word in my heart that I might not sin against you***" (Psalm 119:11).
- Gratitude Journaling: "***Enter his gates with thanksgiving***" (Psalm 100:4).
- Visualization of God's promises: "***Now faith is confidence in what we hope for and assurance about what we do not see***" (Hebrews 11:1).
- Physical Exercise as worship: "***Offer your bodies as a living sacrifice, holy and pleasing to God***" (Romans 12:1).

- Mindful Breathing with the name of Jesus: *"The name of the Lord is a strong tower; the righteous run to it and are safe"* (Proverbs 18:10).
- Creative Expression: pouring out your heart like David in the Psalms.
- Biblical Affirmations spoken aloud: *"Let the weak say, 'I am strong'"* (Joel 3:10), "I am a child of God," "I am more than a conqueror," "His grace is sufficient for me."

When life feels completely out of control, remember: nothing is impossible with God (Luke 1:37). Surround yourself with people who will speak life over you, join a support group, see a counselor if needed, and keep showing up. *"Let us not become weary in doing good, for at the proper time we will reap a harvest if we do not give up"* (Galatians 6:9).

Renewing our minds is one of the most practical, powerful gifts God has given us. With the right support and consistent practice, we train our brains to dwell on what is true, noble, right, pure, lovely, and admirable (Philippians 4:8).

It is an ongoing journey that requires patience, persistence, and compassion for ourselves, but the destination is the peace that surpasses understanding and the abundant life Jesus died to give us.

So how do we renew our minds? The paths are many, but the power is one: the Holy Spirit working through our obedience.

In the next chapter we will discover how to move from simply renewing our minds to actually mastering them—learning to replace or interrupt toxic thoughts the moment they arise, until we live in the freedom and victory Christ has already won for us: *"It is for freedom that Christ has set us free"* (Galatians 5:1). The renewed mind is just the beginning. The mastered mind is where we walk as more than conquerors every single day.

BRAIN **DUMPING**

Our minds can feel like a jumbled mess sometimes, with thoughts racing through them all the time. It makes it hard to pay attention or do something. It feels like a battle just to make one choice.

There are good, bad, harmful, and helpful thoughts all at once on the mind screen, and we don't know where to look or what to do first. ***"We demolish arguments and every pretension that sets itself up against the knowledge of God, and we take captive every thought to make it obedient to Christ"*** (2 Corinthians 10:5).

One of my close friends, recently went through a divorce and was also having money problems. He had problems in his personal life, which affected his work and social life as well. He lost his job and felt like his friends didn't want to be around him. He was having trouble keeping track of everything he needed to do because he was so stressed and overwhelmed. He was always worried about what he had to do, which made it hard for him to focus on his life as a whole. He was about to start using drugs, but luckily he came up with a new idea called brain dumping.

My friend started brain dumping to get all of his thoughts and things to do out of his head and onto paper. After one try, he felt less anxious and stressed and more relaxed and focused. So he made it a part of his daily life. Every day, he would sit down for 10 to 15 minutes and write down everything that was on his mind, like problems he was having now, projects he was working on, goals and dreams he had, and anything else that came to mind.

At first, my friend had a hard time writing everything down because there was so much to remember! But as he kept doing brain dumping, he found that it got easier and easier. He also discovered that it was very helpful in lowering his levels of stress and anxiety.

He was able to get everything out of his head and onto paper instead of always worrying about what he had to do. This helped him concentrate on the good things in his life and feel like he was in charge of his life: "*You will keep in perfect peace those whose minds are steadfast, because they trust in you*" (Isaiah 26:3).

Over time, my friend realized that brain dumping was an important part of his daily life. He kept using it in his personal and professional life and beyond to help him relax and stay on top of his goals and to-dos.

Brain dumping was an easy but effective way for my friend to stay on track, get things done, and stay grounded. You can also take charge of your life and become what you always wanted to be, just like my friend.

So, get a pen and some paper and let's talk about brain dumping. Brain dumping is a way to get all of your thoughts down on paper and clear your mind. It's a great way to lower stress and anxiety and boost focus and productivity.

Brain dumping is a very important technique that has helped millions of people all over the world deal with stress and stay organized. And if it could help other people, why not try it? It might be the answer to all of our problems: *"Cast all your anxiety on him because he cares for you"* (1 Peter 5:7).

Let me tell you about my journey and how writing everything down opened my third eye. I used to be a very stressed out person. I had a lot going on: work, school, deadlines, friends, raising seven children, pastoring, running a Bible College and more.

And I always had the feeling that I was missing something or not keeping up. It was too much for me and was hurting my mental health. I learned about brain dumping one day. It's basically just writing down everything that's on your mind, like your goals, tasks, worries, and everything else.

So, I made the decision to try it. It was hard to write everything down at first. There was just too much! But as soon as I started, it was like a dam broke. I wrote and wrote until everything that was in my head was on the page. And you know what? It felt like a burden had been taken off my shoulders: *"Come to me, all you who are weary and burdened, and I will give you rest"* (Matthew 11:28).

I could see everything I needed to do all of a sudden, and I didn't think I would forget anything important.

After that, I started brain-dumping on a regular basis. When I was feeling stressed or overwhelmed, I would sit down and write down everything that was on my mind. And you know what? It really did help. I was able to keep track of my tasks and to-dos, and I didn't feel like I was drowning in stress anymore.

Now, brain dumping is just something I do every day. It's a simple but useful method that keeps me organized, focused, and grounded. If you're feeling stressed or overwhelmed, I really think you should give it a try: *"Do not be anxious about anything, but in every situation, by prayer and petition, with thanksgiving, present your requests to God. And the peace of God, which transcends all understanding, will guard your hearts and your minds in Christ Jesus"* (Philippians 4:6-7).

The digital world we live in is fast-paced and competitive. We have to make decisions quickly and get things done as quickly as we can. And if we keep working like robots, one day the stress will get too much for us and we could have a nervous breakdown.

Before it's too late, use brain dumping to prevent problems instead of fixing them! Brain dumping is a simple but powerful way to lower stress and anxiety, boost focus and productivity, and stay on top of things.

Brain dumping is basically the process of writing down or typing out everything that's on your mind. It's like giving your brain a big dump. You know how there are times when you have a million thoughts racing through your head and it's hard to concentrate?

Brain dumping helps you get rid of all those thoughts so you can focus better: "***Set your minds on things above, not on earthly things***" (Colossians 3:2).

You can do it very easily with just a pen and paper, or you can use a computer or phone app if you want. Write down everything that comes to mind, no matter how big or small. It could be a chore you have to do, something that's been bothering you, or even just a random thought that came to mind.

Once you've written everything down, you can sort your thoughts into groups (like work, personal, etc.) and decide what you need to do first.

Brain dumping is a great way to relieve stress and anxiety and make it easier to concentrate on what you need to do. And it's very satisfying to check things off your list as you finish them!

So the next time you feel like you have too much on your mind or are stressed out, grab a piece of paper and let your thoughts flow. It could be just what you need to get your mind clear and get things done: "***Write the vision; make it plain on tablets***" (Habakkuk 2:2).

Freewriting is one way to brain dump. Set a timer for 10 to 20 minutes and write nonstop during that time. Don't worry about spelling, grammar, or punctuation. The point is to write down your thoughts without holding back.

Mind mapping is another one. You write your main idea or topic in the middle of a page and then add related ideas and concepts around it. You can make your mind map look better and easier to remember by using colours and shapes.

You can also use listing as a way to brain dump. This means making a list of all the thoughts and ideas that come to mind about a certain issue or subject. You can make your list more organized by using bullet points or numbers.

You could also choose clustering, which is like mind mapping but a little less structured. You start with a main idea and then draw lines out to other ideas and concepts that are related to it. You write these down around the main idea. You can keep clustering until you have a web of ideas that are all related.

Another way to dump your thoughts is to write in a stream of consciousness style, like the one above. This means writing down whatever comes to mind without worrying about how it fits together or makes sense. You keep writing until you feel like you've said everything you need to say.

And last but not least, everyone's favourite: sticky notes. You can use sticky notes to get your thoughts out of your head. Write down each idea or thought on a sticky note, and then group them by theme or similarity. This can be a great way to put your thoughts and ideas in order in your mind.

Brain dumping is a great way to get your thoughts out of your head and onto the page in general. Don't worry about organizing or structuring your thoughts at first; just let them flow. After you've dumped your thoughts out, you can go back and put them in a way that makes more sense: *"**Commit to the Lord whatever you do, and he will establish your plans**"* (Proverbs 16:3).

The idea behind brain dumping is that it can be hard to concentrate and get things done when you have a lot on your mind. When we have a lot of worries, thoughts, and things to do, it can be hard to stay on track and prioritize.

Writing down everything that's on our minds can help us clear out our mental clutter and make room in our brains for more important things: *"**Finally, brothers and sisters, whatever is true, whatever is noble, whatever is right, whatever is pure, whatever is lovely, whatever is admirable—if anything is excellent or praiseworthy—think about such things**"* (Philippians 4:8).

Pick a time of day when you won't be disturbed and can only think about brain dumping. You can do this in the morning, at night, or whenever else works for you.

The most important thing is that you have a place to write things down. Put down everything that's in your head. This can be anything and everything, like tasks, to-dos, worries, goals, ideas, and so on. At this point, don't worry about putting things in order or making a list of what's most important. Just write down everything that comes to mind. Now go over what you've done and put it in order.

After you write everything down, take a few minutes to read it over. Next, put your thoughts into groups, like work, personal, health, etc., and rank the tasks that are most important. And now is the time to act. You can now start taking action because you have a clear picture of everything you need to do.

Start with the most important things and then move on to the others. Don't be afraid to change your priorities as needed and cross off tasks as you finish them.

One of the best things about brain dumping is that you can change it to fit your needs. Some people like to do a brain dump every day as part of their morning or evening routine. Others only do it when they need to.

You can also try out different tools and formats to see which ones work best for you. Some people like to use diagrams or mind maps to organize their thoughts, while others like to use a list. But the goal is still the same: clear your mind and do the most important things first!

Brain dumping looks so easy, and you might not believe it at first. But trust me, it's worth a shot! Brain dumping can be as easy as making a list of things to do or as hard as writing a full-length essay or article.

Brain dumping has many benefits that can help you be more productive, creative, and focused in your everyday life, no matter what form it takes.

One of the best things about brain dumping is that it helps you get rid of mental clutter. Our brains are always getting new information and stimuli, which can make us feel overwhelmed and stressed.

Writing down everything that's on your mind for a few minutes can help you feel less anxious and stressed and clear your mind: *"**Be still, and know that I am God**"* (Psalm 46:10). It's easier to sort and have peace when you can see them all at once.

Brain dumping should be a regular part of your life for another reason: it can help you remember things better. When you write something down, you make a picture of it that you can look at later. This can be very helpful for keeping track of important dates, deadlines, and meetings. You can make a place to store information that you can access at any time by keeping a brain dump journal or digital document.

Brain dumping can also help you see patterns and themes in your thoughts and ideas. It's easier to see how your thoughts are related when you write them all down in one place. You might notice patterns or ideas that keep coming up that you didn't see before. This can be very helpful for coming up with new ideas or solving problems. You can learn more about how you think and come up with better ways to solve problems and make decisions by looking for patterns in your thoughts.

Brain dumping can also help you get more done, which is another great benefit. It can be hard to concentrate on one thing when you have a lot on your mind.

Brain dumping can help you get rid of distractions and concentrate on what you need to do. You can make progress toward your goals in a more organized and effective way by breaking up big projects into smaller tasks and making a list of things to do. This can help you feel less overwhelmed and more accomplished: *"I can do all this through him who gives me strength"* (Philippians 4:13). You can also stop putting things off.

A lot of us put off doing things because we don't know where to start or because we feel like there's too much to do. Brain dumping can help you relax and make tasks easier to handle.

One thing I want to tell you is that this is a great technique that is good for both your mental and physical health. It clears your mind, improves your health, and is a great way to relieve stress. When you're feeling stressed and anxious, writing down everything can help you feel more in charge of your thoughts and lower those feelings of stress and anxiety.

Brain dumping can even help you come up with new ideas! Writing down all your thoughts can help you see things in a new way when you're stuck in a mental rut. You might even think of some completely new ideas that you wouldn't have thought of otherwise.

Brain dumping is also a great way to figure things out. It's not always easy to think clearly when you have a problem. But if you write down the problem and break it down into smaller pieces, you can think of possible solutions and make a plan of action.

Brain dumping can really help you reach your goals if you're trying to set some for yourself. Writing down your goals and dreams makes them more real and possible. You are more likely to reach them because you can see them right in front of you: *"**Delight yourself in the Lord, and he will give you the desires of your heart**"* (Psalm 37:4).

Brain dumping is a way to take care of yourself. Writing down your thoughts and feelings is like giving yourself a hug. It's a way to recognize your feelings and look out for yourself.

And last but not least, brain dumping offers another miracle. This is what it can do: take away the bad thoughts and let the good ones bloom. Brain dumping is a great way to start brain weeding, which is the process of getting rid of thoughts that aren't helpful or useful and clearing out our minds.

When you write down everything that's on your mind, you're taking those thoughts out of your head and putting them on paper or a digital device. This clears your mind and helps you see your thoughts more clearly. You can start to look at and think about your thoughts once you've written them all down. You might notice that some of your thoughts are the same over and over again or don't help you.

Brain weeding is the process of judging your thoughts. It means figuring out what thoughts and beliefs are keeping you from moving forward and getting rid of them: *"**Do not conform to the pattern of this world, but be transformed by the renewing of your mind**"* (Romans 12:2).

Brain dumping is a great way to weed out bad thoughts because it lets us see them clearly. We can make more room in our minds for good thoughts and ideas by getting rid of bad ones. This can help us be healthier and happier overall, as well as boost our creativity and productivity.

So if you're feeling overwhelmed or stuck in negative thought patterns, don't think twice about brain dumping. It's the first step toward brain weeding. It could be the thing you need to clear your head and find more peace and clarity: "***The Lord gives strength to his people; the Lord blesses his people with peace***" (Psalm 29:11).

To keep your mind clean and free of negative thoughts, you need to get rid of the ones that aren't useful. This will help your brain process information better. Taking care of your mind makes it easier to live your life and stay away from bad neurovegetative symptoms: "***Above all else, guard your heart, for everything you do flows from it***" (Proverbs 4:23).

The next time you think your brain is a mess, get a pen and paper or your phone and start writing down everything that's on your mind. It doesn't have to be perfect or look good; just get everything out of your head and onto the page. You might be surprised by how much it can help. Don't forget that taking care of your mental health is important. Make brain dumping a regular part of your self-care routine. Happy dumping!

MIND **BURNOUT**

I once believed burnout was the proof I was serving God with everything I had. I pastored a church, ran a Bible College, counselled people, sometimes till midnight, try to spend time with Kathleen and our seven children, visit my parents and in-laws, speak at events and churches, answered texts at 1 a.m., and told myself exhaustion was a spiritual gift. I even bragged about it.

Then one morning in 2018, my mind went completely blank. My chest tightened so hard I thought I was having a heart attack. Tears rolled down my face after a counsel session with my client. I could hear myself saying, "I can't do this," and walked to the bathroom and sat in a daze. That was the day Jesus broke my idol of performance I was trying to impress.

I spoke to a friend who said acute burnout and adrenal crash. Jesus simply repeated the invitation He had been whispering for years: *"Come to me, all you who are weary and burdened, and I will give you rest. Take my yoke upon you and learn from me, for I am gentle and humble in heart, and you will find rest for your souls*" (Matthew 11:28-29). I finally said yes.

That collapse became the doorway to the freest, most fruitful years of my life, and everything I'm about to share with you I first lived through myself, one trembling step at a time.

A few days before everything shifted, I found myself slipping into a very dark and heavy place inside. All that kept circling in my mind was, "If life is only endless work with no real breakthrough in sight, is it even worth living?"

From as far back as 1997, I had trained myself to live at a high level of stress—juggling work, family, church leadership, and returning to university. My brain had grown so accustomed to constant pressure that rest, true rest, simply wasn't part of who I was.

Over the years we eventually handed the church over and transitioned our Bible-school students to a Christian university we partnered with. I stepped into mental-health work, and doors kept opening—opportunities that felt like blessings. But instead of creating balance, I just poured every ounce of myself into the new career. I used up all my vacation and sick days because the income was good and the sense of purpose was strong.

In the rush, little things fell away. I stopped maintaining my vehicles properly, and within six months two of them suffered the exact same failure—lack of oil—and needed complete engine replacements.

I can see now that God was promoting me, lifting me higher in my calling, yet I wasn't doing for myself what Jesus so wisely did: stepping away to recharge, to pray, to care for my own heart and mind.

One evening I came home exhausted and looked up the staircase. There stood our six daughters and one son—all teenagers, so tall and radiant—and for a moment I thought, "Who are these beautiful young women?"

It broke my heart to realise I had missed so much of their growing up. In that moment I knew something had to change; I couldn't keep pouring from an empty cup.

We took our very first family cruise that year. It was pure joy—laughter, sunshine, memories—but when we returned, I slipped right back into the same relentless rhythm.

Then in 2016 came the tragedy that shook me to my core: a young man at the psychiatric unit I worked at took his life, hanging himself in the bathroom. The weight of that loss settled deep in my soul and added another layer of grief and stress I carried.

I had a leadership role as a professional practice leader, overseeing more than sixty staff while still carrying my full clinical role in the psychiatric unit.

In 2018 a psychologist sought me out and invited me into the field of psychology. On the outside everything looked like favour and forward motion, but between 2017 and 2018 the exhaustion finally overtook me.

My mind slid into a terrifying darkness. Thoughts of suicide began to form—not just fleeting thoughts, but actual plans. Yet every single time, my heart would whisper, "This would devastate your wife and your children. They need you."

I understand that severe burnout can pull a person into such profound depression that life loses its colour and purpose feels impossible to find.

For years I measured success by how little sleep I could survive on and how many plates I could keep spinning. I wore fatigue like a crown.

I thought if I ever slowed down the whole kingdom would stall. Then I discovered Jesus did some of His greatest miracles and then immediately withdrew to solitary places to pray and rest (Luke 5:15-16).

After feeding five thousand He made the disciples get in a boat and sent the crowds away so He could go up the mountain alone (Matthew 14:22-23).

Even on the night He was betrayed He still took time to eat supper slowly, wash feet, and sing a hymn with His friends. Nothing about Jesus' life looked frantic.

I asked God a question: *"Lord, what does success actually look like for me?"* The answer that settled in my spirit was gentle but revolutionary: Success is finishing the race I marked out for myself with joy still in my heart and strength still in my body (Hebrews 12:1-2; Acts 20:24).

I started to develop a routine that fit my schedule, keeping weekends off just to be with the family. The first month felt like rebellion. I kept waiting for lightning to strike. Instead, something better happened: my soul began to breathe again. I slept without an alarm. I took my children to the park and sat on the grass doing absolutely nothing productive.

I read novels. I napped. And on Monday morning I felt better than I ever had when I was exhausted. Psycholgy was leading me down the same path with 37 to 40 clients a week. Evently, I went to three days a week, 24 to 26 clients a week.

I also started asking one brutal question before I said yes to anything: "Ten years from now, will this help me cross the finish line still in love with Jesus and still in love with my family, or will it leave me limping and bitter?" That question has set me free more times than I can count.

Burnout, I learned the hard way, is almost never about the work itself. It's about the lies I was believing while I did the work. My mind had become a prison, and I was both the inmate and the jailer.

The loudest lies were these: "If I don't do it, it won't get done." "Good Christians never say no." "Rest is for people who aren't serious about eternity." "My worth is tied to what I produce." "God loves me more when I'm busy." "No rest for the righteous."

Every one of those thoughts are twisted. So I started doing war the way Paul taught: *"We demolish arguments and every pretension that sets itself up against the knowledge of God, and we take every thought captive to make it obedient to Christ"* (2 Corinthians 10:5). I stopped fighting demons in the heavenlies and started fighting the lies in my own head.

Here's what I did every single day for a year, and still do most days. I sat down with a cheap spiral notebook and dumped every racing thought onto the page for ten minutes (no filter, no editing). Then I drew a line down the middle of the next page. On the left I wrote the lie. On the right I wrote the truth from Scripture that demolished it.

Lie: I'm letting God down if I rest.

Truth: *"The Sabbath was made for man, not man for the Sabbath"* (Mark 2:27) and *"It is finished"* (John 19:30).

Lie: My value comes from my productivity.

Truth: *"You are not your own; you were bought at a price"* (1 Corinthians 6:19-20) and *"The Lord takes delight in his children"* (Psalm 149:4).

Lie: If I say no, people will stop loving me.

Truth: *"Let your yes be yes and your no be no"* (Matthew 5:37) and *"Man looks at the outward appearance, but the Lord looks at the heart"* (1 Samuel 16:7).

I read those pages out loud. Faith comes by hearing (Romans 10:17), especially when the voice you hear is your own declaring God's Word over your own life.

One winter morning in 2018 I was so buried in shame that I could barely get out of bed. I forced myself into the shower and started speaking the truth anyway: "***There is now no condemnation for those who are in Christ Jesus***" (Romans 8:1).

I said it out loud at least fifty-three times that morning—I actually counted—until the tears slowly changed from burning shame to something softer, almost like relief. Speaking it into the light, over and over, took away the lie's grip. By refusing to let it hide in the dark anymore, I finally began to set myself free.

I still keep a stack of 3×5 cards in my car, on my desk, and beside my bed. Each one has a promise. When anxiety whispers, I pull out the card and read it out loud until my body believes what my spirit already knows.

Mental freedom is not the absence of hard thoughts; it is the practiced habit of answering them with a louder truth.

There is a joy that only shows up on the other side of a managed mind. I discovered it the first time I did a weekend conference after my collapse. I had slept eight hours the night before. I had said no to three "urgent" requests that week. I had spent an hour the day before walking in the woods (forest bathing) quoting Psalm 23 out loud.

When I stepped onto the platform that weekend I wasn't running on caffeine and adrenaline. I was running on rest and joy. The message flowed. People wept. I finished strong and still had energy to be with my kids afterward. I cried in the car on the way home, not from exhaustion this time, but from gratitude. This is what it feels like to be alive.

Joy is the serious business of heaven. The joy of the Lord is not a bonus feature for super-spiritual people; it is the fruit of a mind that stays on Him (Isaiah 26:3). "***You make known to me the path of life; in your presence there is fullness of joy; at your right hand are pleasures forevermore***" (Psalm 16:11).

I spent years chasing impact while forfeiting joy. Now I chase His presence, and the impact follows like a shadow.

I started noticing the difference in little things. I laugh louder and longer than I used to. I can sit through an entire movie with my wife without checking my phone. I dance in the kitchen while cooking dinner. I cry at commercials (the happy kind of tears). My daughters says, "Daddy's eyes smile now." That is the return on investment of a managed mind.

The greatest surprise of recovery was discovering that my burnout-proof future was built one tiny obedient choice at a time.

I said no to the 10 p.m. meetings and went to bed instead. I turned my phone on 'Do Not Disturb' after 8 p.m. and the sky did not fall.

I scheduled a weekly date night with Kathleen and protected it like it was a board meeting with Jesus. I started taking a two full day off every week, travel to speaking engaements on weekends and discovered the practice kept growing, never short of clients. I started to hired clincans and admitted I didn't have it all together. I started lifting weights again, ging to the gym 4-5 days a week, eating vegetables, and drinking water like a responsible adult.

Each choice felt insignificant in the moment, but they compounded like interest in a savings account I didn't know I had.

Today I speak better, love deeper, sleep eight hours, and still have margin to write books, visit my paprents and sibligs, spend time with close friends, spend time with the children (6 married; spend a night away with each couple), and quality time with Kathleen. My marriage is stronger than ever. My joy is steady. My health is restored. And I have not had a single panic attack in four years.

People ask me all the time, "How did you do it?" My answer is always the same: I believed Jesus when He said "***His yoke is easy and His burden is light***" (Matthew 11:30). I stopped trying to carry the world on my shoulders and let Him carry both me and the world.

This is not a fantasy. This is my actual life, and it can be yours too.

You do not have to choose between loving God deeply and living sustainably. You do not have to sacrifice your health on the altar of ministry or hustle. The same Spirit who raised Jesus from the dead lives in you, and He is not in a hurry (Romans 8:11). He will finish what He started in you (Philippians 1:6), and He will do it at a pace that leaves you more alive, not less.

So take a deep breath, right now. Let your shoulders drop. Close your eyes and hear Jesus say it again: *"Are you tired? Worn out? Burned out on religion? Come to me. Get away with me and you'll recover your life. I'll show you how to take a real rest. Walk with me and work with me, watch how I do it. Learn the unforced rhythms of grace"* (Matthew 11:28-29, The Message).

That invitation still stands. Say yes today. Your burnout does not get the final word. Jesus does. And He is gentle. And He is enough. And He will lead you all the way home, laughing, rested, and free.

THINK TANDEM

The word "tandem" comes from Latin and literally means "at length" or "one behind the other." It was first used for a carriage pulled by horses harnessed in a single line rather than side by side. Today we use "tandem" whenever two things—people, ideas, or forces—work closely together, supporting and strengthening one another.

The Bible is full of this principle: "***Two are better than one, because they have a good return for their labor. If either of them falls down, one can help the other up***" (Ecclesiastes 4:9-10). "***Though one may be overpowered, two can defend themselves. A cord of three strands is not quickly broken***" (Ecclesiastes 4:12).

Tandem thinking simply means deliberately holding two perspectives, truths, or ideas side by side—often opposing ones—so that fresh insight, wisdom, and healing can emerge. It is the mental version of iron sharpening iron (Proverbs 27:17).

We all have seasons when life feels impossible. I certainly did.

In 2016, a patient hang himself at my workplace and with the stress and chaos, along with many other added stressors, I hit rock bottom. My mind was locked in one gear: "Everything is hopeless. You'll never recover." I couldn't see a way forward. One night a close friend called and said, "Let's try something. I'm going to speak the worst-case scenario, and you speak the best-case scenario—at the same time. No arguing, just hold both truths in tandem."

At first it felt ridiculous, but as we talked, something shifted. By forcing my brain to voice both "This could ruin me" and "*God still has a plan for good*" (Jeremiah 29:11), the stranglehold of despair loosened. Within weeks I had a new job and a repayment plan. That was my first experience of tandem thinking pulling me out of a mental pit.

Tandem thinking is powerful because it reflects how God often works. He holds justice and mercy, sovereignty and human responsibility, grief and hope in perfect tension. "*The Lord is gracious and compassionate, slow to anger and rich in love*" (Psalm 145:8) while still being the righteous Judge. When we learn to think the way God thinks—holding apparent opposites in tension—we begin to see solutions we were blind to before.

Let me tell you about the second time tandem thinking saved me.

In 1990, three weeks before my wedding, panic hit hard. One voice screamed, "You're going to fail her. Run!" The other voice whispered, "God gave her to you as a gift." I was stuck in a civil war inside my own head.

One night I sat on the bathroom floor and forced myself to speak both fears out loud—then immediately speak the opposing truth from Scripture: Fear: "I'm not man enough." Truth: "*I can do all this through Christ who gives me strength*" (Philippians 4:13). Fear: "I'll ruin her life." Truth: "*There is now no condemnation for those who are in Christ Jesus*" (Romans 8:1).

I went back and forth for an hour. Something broke. The fear didn't vanish overnight, but by holding both voices in tandem instead of letting one dominate, I walked down the aisle in peace. My wife and I just celebrated our thirty-five wedding anniversary (2025)—proof that tandem thinking can heal even pre-wedding terror.

Here's how tandem thinking works in everyday life:

You and a trusted partner (spouse, friend, mentor, therapist) sit down with a problem. One person voices one perspective; the other voices the opposite or complementary one. You keep talking until a third, wiser way emerges. Even when you're alone, you can do it: speak the lie, then immediately speak the truth; voice the fear, then voice the promise. *"Take every thought captive to obey Christ"* (2 Corinthians 10:5) often looks exactly like this.

Some practical ways to practice tandem thinking:

- Mind Mapping: Put the problem in the center, then branch out with both positive and negative possibilities.
- SWOT Analysis (Strengths, Weaknesses, Opportunities, Threats) – pure tandem thinking on paper.
- Six Thinking Hats: Force yourself to look at the situation through six different lenses (facts, emotions, caution, benefits, creativity, process).
- Role-playing: Argue with yourself as both the critic and the encourager.
- Journaling two columns: "What my fear says" and "What God's Word says."

I still use a solo version almost every day. When anxiety whispers, "This won't work out," I write it down—then immediately write the tandem truth beside it: *"And we know that in all things God works for the good of those who love him"* (Romans 8:28). The two columns sitting side by side do something chemical in my brain: peace rises, creativity returns, and solutions appear.

Tandem thinking heals the mind because it breaks the tyranny of the single story. Depression and anxiety love to tell one story only: "It will always be this bad." Tandem thinking forces the other story into the light: "*The Lord is close to the brokenhearted and saves those who are crushed in spirit*" (Psalm 34:18) and "*Joy comes in the morning*" (Psalm 30:5).

So here's the invitation:

Next time you feel stuck, overwhelmed, or hopeless, don't fight with just one half of your mind. Invite the other half to the table. Speak the fear—then speak the promise. Write the lie—then write the truth. Call a friend and say, "Will you hold the opposite perspective with me for ten minutes?" Watch what happens when two truths pedal in tandem.

Because the God who spoke light into darkness still loves to take two opposing realities—death and life, mourning and dancing, Good Friday and Easter Sunday—and weave them into resurrection.

You don't have to think alone anymore. Think in tandem—with a friend, with Scripture, with the Holy Spirit—and watch your mind begin to heal.

UNDERSTANDING
THE MIND

AN

affected

There are days I still hear the echo of the hospital halls—the soft hum of machines, the hurried footsteps, and the fragile sound of someone weeping behind a curtain. Working in psychiatry as a crisis intervention specialist, both in the emergency department and alongside the police, has allowed me to witness the rawest corners of the human mind. In those spaces, stripped of pretense and pride, you see what happens when life presses too hard and the mind can no longer carry the weight.

I have seen minds on fire—not with fever, but with exhaustion. There was the young nurse who sat quietly in the staff lounge, her body upright but her spirit collapsed after endless double shifts.

There was the man the police brought in after days of wandering, frightened and disoriented, his thoughts tangled like threads in a storm.

And the mother who couldn't stop crying because her mind would not stop thinking. Her words trembled as she said, "It just won't turn off."

In moments like those, I am reminded of the Psalmist's words: *"My soul is weary with sorrow; strengthen me according to your word."* (Psalm 119:28) That weariness is not just of the soul—it's the weight of the affected mind, crying out for rest.

Ambition, in its purest form, is a beautiful force. It pushes us to achieve, to serve, to care, to build. But ambition carries a price, often paid quietly by the mind.

There was a season when I didn't notice my own decline. Long hours blurred into long nights. I was driven by purpose, yet drained by the endless call of duty. My mind was constantly racing—solving, analyzing, absorbing pain that wasn't mine to keep. It was as if my mind had caught fire, burning slowly, quietly.

No one tells you that burnout begins in silence. You think you can push through, that rest can wait. But the more I pushed, the more I realized that the mind, like the heart, has limits. Every small task felt heavy. Every breath came with a sigh. Even peace felt unreachable.

It was then that I began to understand the call in Psalm 46:10: *"Be still, and know that I am God."* Stillness is not weakness—it is healing. It is sacred space for the mind to breathe again.

To manage your mind is to honour that stillness. To avoid burnout is to learn the humility of rest.

The affected mind wears many faces. Sometimes it is the mind wounded by trauma—the teenager who cannot sleep because her memories will not let her rest.

Sometimes it is the veteran who sits in silence, staring at a wall that only he can see. And sometimes it is the professional—the nurse, the teacher, the officer—who smiles all day and collapses in solitude at night.

These are not broken people; they are simply tired souls carrying more than their minds were designed to bear.

I have learned that healing begins long before medication or therapy. It begins with compassion—with the simple act of being seen, heard, and valued. Scripture tells us, *"He heals the brokenhearted and binds up their wounds."* (Psalm 147:3).

I have witnessed this healing take place in quiet moments, when someone finally feels safe enough to speak their truth, or when silence itself becomes prayer.

Our modern world, however, doesn't make healing easy. We are constantly bombarded with information—notifications, news, noise. I call it "brain congestion," when your thoughts pile up like traffic at rush hour.

There were days after long shifts when I would drive home without the radio on, letting the silence clear my mind. It was there, in that gentle quiet, that I realized how much the mind needs space.

Then there is the racing mind—the "brain combustion"—when thoughts ignite like sparks, one after another, and you can't calm the fire.

I have seen this in patients pacing the halls of the hospital at three in the morning, and I have felt it myself in the sleepless hours after a hard night's work. Christ's words echo softly in such moments: *"Come to me, all you who are weary and burdened, and I will give you rest."* (Matthew 11:28) That invitation is not only for the soul; it is also for the mind.

The noise inside our heads can sometimes be louder than the world around us. The *"noisy brain"* fills itself with chatter—the what-ifs, the should-haves, the never-enoughs.

It can drown out joy, prayer, and even reason. When I work alongside the police during crisis calls, I often find myself praying quietly, asking for peace—not just for the person in distress, but for everyone in the room. Peace, even for a few seconds, can quiet the storm. As Scripture promises, *"The peace of God, which transcends all understanding, will guard your hearts and your minds in Christ Jesus."* (Philippians 4:7)

I have come to see that every one of us carries an affected mind at some point in life. It may be weary from service, wounded by loss, or simply overwhelmed by the pace of existence. But the affected mind is not a broken mind. It is a mind that has felt deeply, cared immensely, and tried bravely. It is the mind that reminds us we are human.

To manage your mind and avoid burnouts is not about perfection— it is about awareness. It is learning to notice the signals of fatigue, to honour rest, to seek connection, and to embrace grace.

The world will always ask for more, but God whispers for stillness. And in that stillness, we find not only peace but renewal.

As I walk down the quiet hospital corridors at the end of my shift, I often pause and whisper a simple prayer—not just for the patients, but for all of us who carry the invisible burdens of thought and feeling.

Healing the affected mind begins there, in those small sacred moments of surrender and compassion, where the mind learns to rest and the heart learns to hope again.

The first time I realized my own mind was burning out, I was standing in the emergency department at two in the morning, holding a clipboard I couldn't focus on. The monitors beeped steadily, the fluorescent lights hummed, and I was surrounded by motion—nurses rushing, security officers stationed near the triage doors, a patient shouting somewhere down the hall. Yet in the middle of all that noise, I felt strangely hollow, like I was watching myself from outside my body.

It had been another sixteen-hour shift. I'd already assessed six psychiatric emergencies: a young woman who had overdosed after a breakup, a middle-aged man found wandering traffic lanes, an elderly patient whose dementia had turned violent.

Each story etched itself into my heart like a scar. I remember writing my notes and feeling a heaviness pressing bchind my eyes, not from fatigue alone, but from carrying too many stories that weren't mine to keep.

When you work in mental health, especially in crisis, you learn early that minds can fracture under weight unseen. I used to think I could handle it all—the trauma, the loss, the endless human need that walked through those double doors.

I told myself it was my calling. I prayed for strength each morning before I walked into the hospital, whispering, "Lord, give me grace for whatever comes." And He did. But even grace needs rest.

That night, I caught sight of my reflection in the glass of the nurses' station. My eyes were bloodshot, my shoulders tight, and I looked like someone who hadn't truly rested in weeks. I tried to smile at myself, but it came out thin. A thought flickered: *How can I care for others when I'm quietly breaking?*

I remembered a verse from Isaiah: *"**He gives strength to the weary and increases the power of the weak**."* (Isaiah 40:29) I repeated it under my breath like a lifeline, feeling the words ground me for a moment. Still, I knew I was running on fumes.

Working in psychiatry teaches you a strange kind of intimacy with suffering. You see minds unravel in real time—panic, delusion, despair—and you're expected to step into that chaos and bring calm. But what they don't teach you is how easily that chaos can seep into your own thoughts if you don't guard your spirit.

There was one patient that week I couldn't stop thinking about. He was in his early twenties, brought in by police after he'd been found sitting on a bridge, legs dangling over the edge. When I entered the assessment room, he wouldn't meet my eyes. His voice was flat when he said, "I'm just tired. My mind won't stop. I can't take it anymore."

We talked for nearly an hour. He spoke about his anxiety, his job that demanded perfection, his parents who didn't understand. Every word resonated deeper than I expected. I realized I was listening not only as a clinician but as someone who also knew what it felt like to be consumed by constant mental noise.

When he finally agreed to stay overnight for safety, I walked out of the room and leaned against the wall, breathing deeply. His pain echoed mine. I whispered, *"Lord, help me keep my own mind steady."*

That prayer became a ritual after each case. Because the truth is, working with broken minds can break yours if you're not careful. Compassion fatigue is a real and quiet thief—it doesn't shout, it whispers.

It tells you you're fine, that you're strong, that others have it worse. Until one day you realize your empathy has turned into exhaustion, your patience into numbness, and your calling into a burden.

One evening, after finishing a long shift, I sat in my car in the hospital parking lot and couldn't bring myself to start the engine. My thoughts were a blur of patient names, risk assessments, and unfinished tasks.

I felt like my mind had become an overfilled inbox—too many tabs open, too many alarms ringing. That's when I began to understand the phrase "the affected mind."

An affected mind is not just the patient's mind—it's ours too. It's the mind that gives and listens and carries. It's the mind that tries to fix, even when it's breaking. It's the mind that holds both the suffering of others and its own unspoken ache.

*"**Be still, and know that I am God.**"* (Psalm 46:10) Those words came back to me later that night. Stillness, I realized, is not idleness—it's obedience. It's the pause that allows healing to begin.

Over the years, I learned to recognize the quiet signs of mental fatigue—the shorter temper, the lingering sadness, the inability to sleep even when exhausted, the small window of tolerance.

The brain, when overworked, begins to short-circuit emotionally. You can't pour into others when your own cup is empty.

I began to schedule silence the way others schedule meetings. I would step outside between patient assessments, feel the wind on my face, breathe deeply, and remind myself: *I am not the healer, only a vessel for healing.*

It wasn't easy. Sometimes I failed at it entirely.

One particularly heavy week, we admitted a woman in her forties who had attempted suicide. She'd lost her husband suddenly and felt her world collapse. During our sessions, she often sat silent for long stretches, her hands trembling in her lap. Then one afternoon, she looked up and said, "Do you ever get tired of people like me?"

Her question cut straight through me. I told her, honestly, "No. But I do get tired with you."

She smiled faintly. "That's different."

I nodded. "Yes. It means I'm human too."

After she was discharged weeks later, I thought about that conversation often. We are not called to be invincible. Even Jesus withdrew to lonely places to pray. Even He rested. If the Son of God took time to renew His spirit, how could I believe I was exempt?

In those early years, I was learning that managing the mind isn't about control—it's about compassion. Compassion for others, yes, but also for ourselves. Without that balance, empathy turns into erosion.

When I began working more closely with law enforcement as a mental health specialist, that lesson became even more critical. The streets brought a different kind of noise—sirens, arguments, chaos unfolding in real time.

There were nights when I rode with officers to mental health calls in dark neighbourhoods, unsure what we would find. Sometimes it was a person in deep psychosis, convinced that unseen forces were hunting them. Other times, it was someone standing in the middle of the street, shouting at the stars.

In one case, we arrived at a gas station where a man was pacing barefoot, muttering to himself. When I approached, he stopped and said quietly, "Do you hear them too?"

His eyes were wide, terrified. I shook my head gently. "No, but I believe you hear them."

That acknowledgment—simple, truthful—softened something in him. He allowed us to help him without force. Later, in the back of the ambulance, he whispered, "I just want the voices to stop."

I remember holding his hand and saying, "You're not alone. There's peace for you yet."

"Come to me, all you who are weary and burdened, and I will give you rest." (Matthew 11:28)

That verse has echoed through countless encounters like that. The weary are everywhere—behind locked hospital doors, under highway bridges, in tidy suburban homes. The affected mind wears no single face.

The first time I rode in a patrol car for a mental-health call, the night air felt heavy with uncertainty. The city lights blurred through the windshield, and the radio crackled with calls for service.

Sitting beside an officer I'd come to trust over the years, I realized how different this world was from the hospital. There were no bright lights or medical teams here—only a thin thread of faith holding chaos together.

We arrived at a small apartment complex around 9pm. A neighbour had called about a man screaming that demons were in his home. When we climbed the narrow stairs, the door was already open, and the man stood in the middle of the living room, trembling. The officer nodded at me, stepping back so I could speak first.

"Hi, I'm here to make sure you're okay," I said gently. "Can we talk?"

He looked at me, sweat streaming down his face. "They're in the walls. I can hear them moving."

"I believe you're hearing something that feels real," I replied. "Let's sit for a moment so you can catch your breath."

He hesitated, then lowered himself onto the edge of a sofa. His hands shook. I could feel his fear fill the room. I sat across from him, matching his breathing. Slowly, the tremors subsided. I prayed silently, *Lord, help him feel safe.*

After a few minutes, he whispered, "You're not afraid of me."

"No," I said. "I'm here to help you find peace tonight."

Later, as we transported him to the hospital for evaluation, as he was apprehended under section 17 of the Mental health Act in Ontario. He had made threats to kill himself to get rid of the voices. I treated him like he was my own family member.

I thought of the verse in 1 John 4:18: *"There is no fear in love. But perfect love drives out fear."* Every crisis scene, I realized, was an invitation to practice that kind of love—to enter fear and carry peace into it.

Working in the field with police taught me that mental illness does not always look clinical. Sometimes it looks like a mother sitting in her car, unable to start the engine because anxiety has frozen her body.

Sometimes it looks like a teenager standing on a bridge, tears streaming silently, who wants to kill himself. And sometimes it looks like an officer who has seen too much and doesn't know how to talk about it.

One evening, we responded to a call from a grocery-store parking lot. A young woman was sitting on the curb, clutching a small notebook. The store manager had called because she wouldn't move or speak.

When I approached, she wouldn't look up. I crouched beside her and asked softly, "What's in the notebook?"

She held it out. Inside were pages of tiny writing—her fears, her prayers, her confessions. In shaky letters she had written, *I can't quiet my mind.*

I sat beside her for a long time, reading the words she allowed me to see. Finally I said, "Your mind is talking because it's hurting. But it's still yours. You can learn to care for it, not fight it."

Tears rolled down her cheeks, and she whispered, "Is it really possible?"

"Yes," I said. "You just took the first step by asking for help."

That night stayed with me. When I returned home, I couldn't sleep. I thought about how many of us live with notebooks like hers—pages of thoughts we never show anyone, fears we keep folded inside. The affected mind is often the silent one, the one carrying invisible storms.

In the following months, I began keeping my own small notebook, not of worries but of gratitude. Each night I wrote one thing that reminded me God was still near.

Some days it was as simple as a patient's smile, or a moment of laughter with a weary officer. The practice slowed the rush inside my head.

"Do not be anxious about anything, but in every situation, by prayer and petition, with thanksgiving, present your requests to God." (Philippians 4:6)

Gratitude, I discovered, is medicine for the overworked mind.

Not every call ended peacefully. There were nights filled with grief—scenes that left a mark deeper than I expected. Once, we were dispatched to a call of a fourteen years old male standing in the balcony wanting to jump

I remember being sent to the balcony, the cold wind whipping through my jacket as I stepped toward him, careful not to startle. The officer whispered, "You've got the words. Try." As over ten officers stood watching.

I called out, "My name's — I work with the crisis team. I'm not here to arrest you or to judge you. Can you talk to me?"

He didn't answer. I could see his knuckles against the metal rail. I kept speaking, slowly, rhythmically, the way you would speak to someone lost in a nightmare. "Whatever pain brought you here tonight doesn't have to end this way. You are seen. You are loved. You're not alone."

Minutes felt like hours, but finally he turned his head slightly and said, "Nobody believes that anymore."

"I do," I said simply. I added, "if you jump, I will jump with you and remember I have seven children who will not have a father".

He started to cry, and the tears loosened something—first in him, then in me. When he stepped down and allowed me to take him inside his apartment, I silently thanked God for that small miracle. His parents were not at home, who was informed later that their son had been to be taken to the hospital.

Driving back to the station later, the officer said, "I don't know how you do it. I've seen too many jump."

I answered, "I don't always know either. But I remind myself it isn't me saving anyone. It's grace showing up in time."

That truth became my safeguard. In crisis work, you must remember you're a conduit, not the source. The mind that tries to carry everyone's salvation will collapse under the weight.

There were also quiet victories—the man who stopped drinking after months of outreach visits, the woman who began painting again after years of depression. Healing often came slowly, in tiny increments, like sunlight creeping across a dark room.

During one shift, an officer and I checked on a homeless veteran who had been reported wandering the park talking to unseen companions. We found him sitting beneath a tree, humming softly. I offered him a bottle of water and asked if he'd like to talk. He smiled and said, "You don't have to worry. The angels already came."

I sat with him for nearly thirty minutes as he told stories of his service, of nights sleeping under bridges, of strangers who offered kindness. Before we left, he looked up at the sky and said, "You know, I think my mind got tired before my body did."

Those words followed me home. A tired mind can disguise itself as laziness, irritability, or apathy, but beneath it is often deep fatigue from fighting battles no one sees. The veteran's quiet acceptance reminded me of Psalm 34:18: *"**The Lord is close to the brokenhearted and saves those who are crushed in spirit.**"*

Back at the hospital, the rhythm of inpatient life contrasted with the chaos of the streets. There was structure, routine, medication rounds, therapy groups. Yet the suffering there was just as real.

I learned to notice small things—the way a patient folded paper cranes during visiting hours, the sound of laughter returning to the unit after a hard week. Each moment of hope felt sacred.

One afternoon, I led a group discussion about coping with intrusive thoughts. A young man who had battled obsessive-compulsive disorder raised his hand and said, "My brain's like a radio I can't turn off."

Everyone nodded. I asked them, "What helps you lower the volume, even for a minute?"

Answers came slowly: prayer, music, writing, sitting in sunlight. When it was my turn, I said, "For me, it's remembering I'm not the sum of my thoughts. My mind can be busy, but my spirit can still rest."

That day, after the group ended, one of the patients approached and said, "When you said that, I felt something shift. Like I'm not broken, just tired."

We both smiled. "Tired minds can heal," I told him. "They just need gentleness."

Gentleness—toward others, toward ourselves—became a daily practice. Each morning before walking onto the unit, I whispered a prayer from Lamentations 3:23: *"**His mercies are new every morning**."*

No matter what happened the day before, that verse reminded me there was always another chance to start again.

There were moments of doubt too.

Days when bureaucracy, staff shortages, and the endless cycle of admissions made me wonder if anything truly changed. Managing your mind means allowing renewal even when the world feels unchanged.

As months turned into years, I began to recognize patterns: how stress piled up subtly, how exhaustion disguised itself as drive. I learned that helping others find balance required me to live it first.

I began taking short time away with Kathleen and the children, walking by the ocean, spending time with family without checking my phone. Those moments reminded me that rest is not escape—it's preparation for endurance.

Sometimes I still see the faces of the people we helped on the streets or the patients who waved goodbye from the ward. Their stories linger like quiet prayers. They taught me more about faith and resilience than any textbook ever could.

The affected mind, I've learned, isn't defined by its wounds but by its capacity to seek healing. Each person I've met—officer, patient, stranger—mirrors a truth we all share: the mind is both fragile and resilient, capable of despair and redemption in the same breath.

When I return to Scripture now, verses about peace strike differently. *"You will keep in perfect peace those whose minds are steadfast, because they trust in you."* (Isaiah 26:3)

Trust steadies the mind when the world spins. It doesn't erase the chaos, but it anchors us within it.

I realized that managing the mind isn't just about helping others—it was about helping myself survive the work I loved.

I've learned that acknowledging my own fragility is not weakness—it is life-saving. Psalm 147:3 says, *"He heals the brokenhearted and binds up their wounds."*

I thought about how many patients I had watched through broken nights, and suddenly, I understood that healing begins with honesty: admitting our minds are affected, wounded, even exhausted.

I began to build practices that grounded me in the storms. Every morning, before the chaos of the hospital unit or the unpredictability of a police call, I would spend ten to fifteen minutes in quiet reflection. Sometimes it was prayer, sometimes scripture reading, and sometimes just sitting in silence. On days when the world felt loudest, I found that these moments were islands of calm.

All that ambition comes with a price: the risk of burning out our minds. I remember the first time I felt it in myself, though I didn't know what it was at the time. After months of long hours, pushing my limits in the hospital and on the streets, I felt a heaviness that no coffee or pep talk could fix. My thoughts wouldn't stop racing. Tasks that used to feel manageable now seemed impossible.

The more I tried to push through, the more wounded my mind became. It was like carrying a weight that no one could see, and every small responsibility became an insurmountable obstacle. The constant bombardment of ideas, worries, and memories began to chip away at my mental health.

Some days, I felt as if my brain was in chaos, a storm that I couldn't calm. If I didn't take steps to care for myself, I feared the consequences would be worse than exhaustion—they could be irreversible.

Life has a way of testing our minds every day. Stress from work, family, relationships, poor sleep, unhealthy habits, social media pressure, and even moments of laziness—all these things take a toll.

When we are overwhelmed, it's easy to ignore the signals our minds send. But there are ways to cope. Reaching out for help isn't weakness—it's survival. Your mind will thank you later.

A mind can suffer silently. Even if the body appears fine, constant worry, harsh words, and trauma can wound it. Confusion, lack of focus, and brain fog are common symptoms when the mind is overworked. Like our body, it requires rest and attention. Without care, the damage can be profound.

Faith is a lifeline. I reflected often on Philippians 4:13: *"I can do all things through Christ who strengthens me."*

Over time, I began to understand that strength didn't mean endless endurance without rest. It meant trusting that even when my mind faltered, God's strength would meet me there. Even in the darkest nights, the most chaotic streets, or the most despairing wards, His presence was steady.

Sometimes, healing required small, tangible rituals. After a particularly traumatic weekend, I would go home and write down every thought that lingered, every image I couldn't release. I called it "mind decluttering."

Watching the words appear on the page gave them space to exist without controlling me. By evening, I felt lighter, as though the heaviness of countless crises had been acknowledged and then set down.

There were also moments in nature that I carried into my practice. Walking along a quiet trail, I noticed the gentle sway of trees, the quiet hum of insects, the sunlight filtering through leaves. These small miracles reminded me that the world was still intact, even when the human mind faltered.

Psalm 19:1 came to mind: *"The heavens declare the glory of God; the skies proclaim the work of his hands."* Nature, like scripture, became a mirror for the mind: steady, enduring, full of quiet wisdom.

I also began mentoring newer crisis workers. Watching their faces— the excitement, the fear, the empathy—I remembered my own early days. I taught them what I had learned the hard way: that it is impossible to pour from an empty cup.

You must care for your mind as diligently as you care for others' minds. Some days we would speak about scripture, some days about practical strategies: scheduling breaks, debriefing after calls, practicing mindfulness.

One new officer, after a chaotic night at a downtown shelter in Peel region, confided, "I feel like I'm losing myself in everyone else's pain."

I smiled gently. "You're noticing. That's the first step. Your mind needs boundaries just as much as compassion. Protect it."

We prayed together, briefly, and then I shared a favourite verse: Matthew 11:28, *"Come to me, all you who are weary and burdened, and I will give you rest."*

I reminded them that rest is not failure—it is preparation. The affected mind cannot be ignored; it must be tended like a fragile garden.

Over time, I noticed my own mind stabilizing in ways I hadn't imagined. Burnout moments came, yes, but I could recognize them early. The racing thoughts of brain combustion were tempered by daily reflection.

Brain congestion faded when I practiced deliberate pauses. Even the wounded places—memories of trauma, grief, or helplessness—began to soften with prayer, gratitude, and gentle action.

There were still nights when I returned home exhausted, and my brain felt like it would not quiet. But even then, I found solace in small rituals. Lighting a candle. Listening to soft music.

Reading scripture aloud. Psalm 23 became a nightly companion: *"Even though I walk through the valley of the shadow of death, I will fear no evil, for you are with me."*

Faith, I discovered, does not always remove the darkness—but it makes it tolerable, navigable. It allows the mind to breathe even when chaos is near.

Looking back, I understand now that every patient, every street call, every sleepless night has been part of a larger lesson: the mind is affected not because we are weak, but because we are human.

And human minds, even the strongest, require care, guidance, and rest. To manage your mind is not selfish; it is sacred. It allows you to show up fully for others without losing yourself.

In sharing my stories, my hope is that anyone reading understands this: burnout, woundedness, brain congestion, and combustion are not signs of failure. They are signals—red flags that the mind needs attention.

And when we respond to those signals with gentleness, faith, and practical care, we can emerge not just whole, but resilient.

A

burnout MIND

Our mind is the most beautiful, powerful, and extraordinary gift of God. It is a divine creation, intricately designed, capable of guiding every function in our body. Each thought, emotion, and decision are a testament to its miraculous autonomy.

It controls our cells, dictates the functioning of every organ, and ultimately shapes our destiny. To neglect the mind is to risk the well-being of the entire body, for when the mind suffers, the body cannot perform optimally. Taking care of our mind is not optional—it is an act of stewardship over God's greatest gift.

Yet, despite its strength, the mind is also astonishingly vulnerable. External pressures, internal struggles, trauma, and stressors can overwhelm it. At one moment, it stands as a powerhouse, orchestrating our lives with clarity and precision.

At the next, it may falter, become fragile, and eventually burn out. Burnout is that extreme mental exhaustion that creeps in silently but leaves profound consequences if left unchecked.

I first encountered the depth of burnout in my work in the psychiatric unit. One evening, I was attending to a patient whose anxiety had escalated into complete shutdown. She couldn't speak, couldn't focus, and her eyes held a distant, glazed expression that spoke louder than words. I sat beside her, feeling the weight of her exhaustion, and I realized I had been ignoring my own signs of burnout for months.

The constant pressure to perform, to hold composure, and to offer hope to others had drained me. In that quiet, I whispered a prayer, "Lord, give me strength, and heal the weary mind." Psalm 34:18 came to mind: *"The Lord is close to the brokenhearted and saves those who are crushed in spirit."*

Burnout is subtle in its approach. Some signs are obvious: feeling tired all the time, a decrease in performance, lack of motivation, and detachment from activities once enjoyed. Others are more insidious: irritability, negative self-talk, physical aches, poor sleep, and changes in appetite.

I remember a police officer I worked with during a crisis intervention training. He confided that he hadn't slept more than three hours a night for over a week, juggling emergencies, paperwork, and personal responsibilities. His hands shook slightly as he admitted he couldn't focus anymore. "I just don't care like I used to," he said quietly. The burnout had crept in slowly, silently wearing down his mind, and he didn't notice until it nearly stopped him in his tracks.

Mind burnout, formally known as Burnout Syndrome, is more than mere tiredness. It is mental, emotional, and often physical exhaustion that builds over time. It rarely stems from a single event.

Rather, it is the cumulative effect of stressors—work pressures, relationship struggles, financial concerns, academic expectations, or traumatic experiences.

Like a cup overflowing with water, the mind reaches its limit quietly, until it finally spills over, leaving us drained, anxious, and disconnected.

I have personally walked through burnout. During my years in psychiatric care, the sheer volume of trauma patients and crisis calls tested every fiber of my being. There were nights I returned home with my mind racing uncontrollably. Images of patients in despair, arguments among colleagues, and the raw pain of human suffering played like an endless reel.

I would lie awake, physically exhausted but mentally trapped, feeling a heaviness I couldn't shake. Philippians 4:6-7 became a lifeline: *"Do not be anxious about anything, but in every situation, by prayer and petition, with thanksgiving, present your requests to God. And the peace of God, which transcends all understanding, will guard your hearts and your minds in Christ Jesus."*

I learned to hand over my worries to God, recognizing that carrying them alone was unsustainable.

One of the most profound causes of burnout is overthinking. Our minds are extraordinary, capable of processing thousands of thoughts daily. But when every situation, past event, or future uncertainty becomes a subject of obsessive thought, mental energy depletes rapidly.

I once had a patient who could not sleep because he was replaying a single confrontation at work over and over. His mind was exhausted from constant vigilance, worry, and self-criticism.

I told him that I surrender my control to God's hands, as he had asked how I manage my mental health. I shared Proverbs 3:5-6: *"Trust in the Lord with all your heart and lean not on your own understanding; in all your ways submit to him, and he will make your paths straight.*" Letting go of the illusion of control was transformative for him—and for me as I guided him.

Expectations, both internal and external, are another heavy burden on the mind. Unrealistic expectations from family, colleagues, or even ourselves can deplete our mental reserves.

I remember a young nurse in the psychiatric unit who held herself to impossible standards. Every mistake, no matter how small, weighed on her mind like a boulder. She would skip meals, forgo sleep, and push herself beyond her limits.

Over time, burnout manifested: fatigue, forgetfulness, emotional volatility, and a sense of hopelessness. I shared Matthew 11:28-30 with her: *"Come to me, all you who are weary and burdened, and I will give you rest. Take my yoke upon you and learn from me, for I am gentle and humble in heart, and you will find rest for your souls. For my yoke is easy and my burden is light."* She had asked how I take care of my mental health. In that moment, she allowed herself to pause, to breathe, and to trust that perfection was not required.

Burnout doesn't just affect thoughts—it reshapes the brain. Chronic stress triggers the release of cortisol, the stress hormone, which, over time, can shrink the hippocampus, impairing memory and learning.

It can disrupt the prefrontal cortex, diminishing decision-making and executive function. Sleep deprivation further compounds these effects, leaving the mind foggy and incapable of clear thought.

I have seen this firsthand. Officers returning from long shifts, patients grappling with prolonged stress, and even fellow healthcare workers exhibited slowed cognition, irritability, and emotional detachment. The body feels exhausted, but the mind is the first casualty.

The physical manifestations of burnout are just as telling. Persistent fatigue, muscle aches, digestive problems, and headaches become routine. Emotionally, individuals experience irritability, anxiety, depression, and feelings of worthlessness.

I recall one evening at the hospital when a colleague, a single mother working two jobs, sat slumped in the staff lounge. Her hands trembled, and her eyes were hollow. "I feel like I'm drowning," she whispered. Her mind had been overworked for months, and burnout had overtaken her once vibrant spirit.

I reminded her of God's peace, as she asked "what keeps you happy all the time". Isaiah 40:29-31 resonated deeply: "*He gives strength to the weary and increases the power of the weak. Even youths grow tired and weary, and young men stumble and fall; but those who hope in the Lord will renew their strength. They will soar on wings like eagles; they will run and not grow weary, they will walk and not be faint.*"

Burnout can also strain relationships. Emotional detachment, irritability, and withdrawal often create distance from loved ones.

I remember a colleague in the police force, who had dedicated years to crisis intervention, gradually isolating himself. Friends noticed he rarely smiled, spoke less, and seemed perpetually exhausted.

His mind, overwhelmed by years of trauma exposure, family issues and unrelenting responsibility, needed care he hadn't allowed himself. Unfortunately, later on that year he took his life.

I had to remind myself the need to take care of my mind, memorizing Psalm 23:3: "*He restores my soul. He guides me in paths of righteousness for his name's sake.*" Restoration begins with acknowledging the need for care.

Self-care is not indulgence—it is survival. For me, simple daily practices became anchors against burnout. Writing morning devotions to my children and posting them on social media, taking short walks, prayer, and breathing exercises provided respite.

On nights when my work schedule was overwhelming, I would step outside, feel the air on my face, and recite Psalm 46:10: "*Be still, and know that I am God.*"

Even in chaos, these moments of stillness reminded me that my mind need not carry every burden alone.

Burnout is a warning. It tells us that our minds need rest, our hearts need support, and our souls need God. Ignoring it can lead to severe consequences: depression, anxiety, cognitive impairment, or long-term emotional exhaustion. But, like any warning, it is also an opportunity—a chance to recalibrate, restore, and redirect.

I have seen remarkable recoveries. Once I was on the brink of burnout, when I began setting boundaries at work, dedicating time for prayer, and seeking support from colleagues and therapists. Over months, my energy returned, my focus sharpened, and my joy in serving patients was renewed.

Romans 12:2 became our mantra: *"Do not conform to the pattern of this world, but be transformed by the renewing of your mind. Then you will be able to test and approve what God's will is—his good, pleasing and perfect will."* Transformation is possible when we nurture the mind and trust God's plan.

Our minds, though extraordinary, has limits. Without deliberate attention, rest, and spiritual grounding, burnout is inevitable. Yet, with awareness, care, and God's guidance, the mind can recover, flourish, and thrive.

Ultimately, managing a burnout mind is about recognizing the signs, setting boundaries, seeking help, and relying on God's strength. It is about integrating faith, practical self-care, and community support into daily life. It is about understanding that our minds, like precious vessels, must be protected, nurtured, and renewed.

Psalm 62:1-2 reminds us: *"Truly my soul finds rest in God; my salvation comes from him. Truly he is my rock and my salvation; he is my fortress, I will never be shaken."*

In the valleys of exhaustion, in the storms of overwork, and in the shadows of burnout, we can anchor our minds in God's unwavering love and care.

Raising seven children with my wife Kathleen was one of the most joyous and challenging journeys of my life. Every day, our thoughts were consumed with their needs—the food they would eat, the clothes they would wear, the homework they had, and the lessons we wanted them to learn about life, faith, and love.

It was a beautiful chaos, a symphony of tiny voices, laughter, cries, and endless questions. But amidst all this joy, I began to feel the quiet pressure building inside me.

I would get up before sunrise, often skipping breakfast, to make sure everyone had what they needed. Then the workday would start—a relentless cycle of tasks, meetings, and responsibilities.

I told myself I could handle it all, that as long as my family was cared for, everything else would work itself out. I even used my vacation days and sick leave not to rest, but to catch up on work I couldn't finish during normal hours. My mind felt like a well-oiled machine, running nonstop, but eventually, the oil began to dry up.

There were nights I lay awake, listening to the quiet of our house while Kathleen slept beside me. The children were finally asleep, the chores were done, but my mind refused to rest.

I would replay the day's events over and over: Did I spend enough time with the kids? Did I ensure they had everything they needed? Did I give Kathleen the support she deserved? And then the next day, it all started again. Over time, I realized that in trying to give everything to everyone, I had given nothing to myself.

Psalm 127:3-5 often came to my mind during these times: "***Children are a heritage from the Lord, offspring a reward from him. Like arrows in the hands of a warrior are children born in one's youth. Blessed is the man whose quiver is full of them.***"

I understood that the responsibility I carried was a gift from God, but the gift felt heavy when I tried to carry it alone. I was so focused on providing for my children that I ignored the signals my mind was sending me, the signs that it was close to burning out.

Burnout doesn't arrive with a loud alarm. It creeps in slowly. I started noticing subtle changes: I was irritable with the children, snapping at minor annoyances, feeling impatient when Kathleen asked me simple questions.

My sleep, even when I had the chance, became restless and shallow. My appetite fluctuated; some days I wouldn't eat because I was "too busy," other days I would overeat out of stress. I was constantly drained, yet I convinced myself I had to keep going.

One evening, I remember Kathleen gently placing her hand on mine as we sat at the kitchen table after putting the children to bed. "You can't keep doing this," she said softly. "You're going to burn out." She added, "you need to find a 9-5 job, Monday to Friday".

At that moment, I realized she was right. I had been so focused on taking care of everyone else that I had neglected the one person who needed care the most—myself.

Mark 12:31 echoed in my mind: *"**Love your neighbour as yourself.**"* How could I truly love and provide for my family if I didn't first care for myself?

The next few weeks became a turning point. I had to learn to say no, to set boundaries, and to take time to recharge. I started waking up a little earlier, not to work, but to pray, meditate, and prepare myself mentally for the day.

I began scheduling small breaks throughout the day, moments when I could step outside, feel the sun, and breathe deeply. These moments seemed insignificant at first, but gradually they restored my energy and focus.

It was not long after that conversation, God opened a job for me to work full-time in psychiatry, Monday to Friday 9-5pm.

Raising seven children is a joyful yet exhausting task, and it requires constant presence and energy. I had to remind myself that taking care of my mind was not selfish—it was necessary.

God gave me these children to nurture, guide, and love, but He also gave me His wisdom to protect my own health and mind. Philippians 2:4 became a guiding verse: "*Let each of you look not only to his own interests, but also to the interests of others*." Looking after myself allowed me to better serve Kathleen and our children.

I also realized that burnout can affect even the happiest families. There were days when I was physically present but mentally absent, too exhausted to engage with the kids' stories, to laugh at their jokes, or to comfort them when they were upset.

My love for them didn't disappear, but the mental exhaustion created an invisible wall between us. It was a wake-up call that if I didn't prioritize my mental and emotional well-being, I risked being unable to fully participate in the lives of the children I cherished so much.

The pressure to provide materially, emotionally, and spiritually for seven children can feel overwhelming. I would sometimes sit at my desk after putting the kids to bed, staring at bills, grocery lists, school forms, and my own work emails, thinking, "How am I going to do all of this?"

In those moments, I had to remind myself that God had given me each day one at a time. Matthew 6:34 provided comfort: "*Therefore do not worry about tomorrow, for tomorrow will worry about itself. Each day has enough trouble of its own*."

Focusing on the present, instead of the mountain of responsibilities, allowed me to reclaim some peace in my mind.

One of the hardest lessons was learning to accept imperfection. I wanted everything for my children—the perfect meals, the perfect schooling, the perfect home.

But burnout often arises when expectations exceed what is humanly possible. Over time, I realized that showing up, being present, and loving my children unconditionally mattered far more than perfection.

Romans 8:28 reminded me: *"And we know that in all things God works for the good of those who love him, who have been called according to his purpose."*

Even when I faltered, God's grace allowed me to keep moving forward, slowly healing my mind and restoring my energy.

There were also practical steps I took to prevent my mind from burning out entirely. I involved Kathleen more actively in planning and organizing the children's schedules, shared household responsibilities, and allowed myself to delegate tasks I had once insisted on doing alone.

I made time for exercise, short walks, and occasional quiet moments to read scripture or simply breathe. I began to cherish small victories— the laughter of a child, a moment of quiet reflection, a completed chore—rather than focusing solely on what remained to be done.

Over the years, I discovered that burnout is not a failure of character; it is a signal that our mind, body, and spirit are reaching their limits.

Even a loving, diligent father and husband like myself could reach a point of exhaustion if self-care is ignored.

In my journey, leaning on God's wisdom, leaning on Kathleen's support, and creating intentional rest periods became lifelines. Psalm 23:2-3 resonated deeply: *"He makes me lie down in green pastures, he leads me beside quiet waters, he refreshes my soul."*

I learned that rest is not weakness—it is a divine gift, essential to sustaining the mind and heart for the long journey of raising a family.

In 2017, I made a pivotal shift in my professional journey. After over seventeen years working in the psychiatric unit, one tragic event shook me to my core—a young man in the unit had taken his own life. The grief, the questions, and the haunting "what ifs" clung to my mind.

I loved working in psychiatry, helping people navigate their darkest moments, but that incident made me realize that I needed a change in the way I worked with minds. I needed a role where I could make a difference but also protect my own mental and emotional health. That's when I transitioned into psychology and psychotherapy work.

In my new role, I found deep satisfaction and fulfillment. The first year I went into private practice, I was seeing 35 to 40 clients a week, each session lasting 50 minutes, focusing on helping individuals understand their minds, confront their fears, and heal from trauma.

The work was rewarding, but the demands were intense. Each client required my full attention, empathy, and energy. By the end of the day, my mind felt like it had run a marathon, yet I had to prepare for the next day, ensuring each session was approached with clarity and care.

Despite my best intentions, the relentless schedule began to take its toll. I remember one night vividly, sitting at my desk after seeing my last client, and feeling completely paralyzed. My mind had reached its limit. Thoughts that once came easily were tangled and heavy.

I couldn't focus, I couldn't make decisions, and I felt completely drained. That night, I realized I had hit a point of total burnout.

Psalm 61:2 came to mind: "*From the ends of the earth I call to you, I call as my heart grows faint; lead me to the rock that is higher than I.*" I needed support, guidance, and restoration, and I turned to the ones who knew me best—my family.

I called Kathleen and the children together. We prayed as a family. I shared with them how exhausted my mind felt, how heavy the work had become, and how I could no longer continue at this pace. Their prayers and support were a balm to my weary soul. I realized that even a strong mind, no matter how resilient, can only handle so much before it demands rest and renewal.

After that night, I made a conscious decision to adjust my schedule. I cut my workdays to three per week. Even with this reduction, I continue to see eight to nine clients per day, which was demanding but manageable.

It was a humbling lesson in setting boundaries and protecting my mental health. I had always prioritized my clients' needs, my family's needs, and my professional responsibilities, often at the expense of my own well-being.

But this experience taught me that caring for my mind was not optional—it was necessary for me to continue serving others effectively and being present for my family.

Balancing psychotherapy work and raising seven children required intentional planning and support. Kathleen became my anchor. We coordinated schedules, divided responsibilities, and made sure that even in my busiest work periods, I had time to be present with the children—helping with homework, attending school events, and sharing meals together.

I learned to cherish these moments, realizing that the love and attention I gave my children was more than just a duty—it was nourishment for both them and me.

Psalm 46:1-2 became a constant source of comfort: *"**God is our refuge and strength, an ever-present help in trouble. Therefore we will not fear, though the earth give way and the mountains fall into the heart of the sea**."*

Even in the chaos of back-to-back client sessions, household responsibilities, and parenting challenges, I could find a sense of peace knowing that God was present in every moment, guiding and sustaining me.

One of the hardest lessons was learning to say no, not out of selfishness, but out of necessity. I had to stop taking on additional clients when my schedule was full, to protect my energy and my mental clarity.

I had to embrace imperfection—realizing that I could not save every soul, fix every problem, or control every outcome. This was a crucial step in preventing a deeper, more destructive burnout.

Even with these adjustments, some days were still hard. I would come home after a long day, exhausted both mentally and physically, and feel guilty for not being able to give my full attention to the children.

But Kathleen would gently remind me: "You are doing enough. You are showing them what dedication and resilience look like, and that's enough."

Her words, coupled with our family prayers, reminded me that restoration is not a single event but an ongoing practice of care, faith, and balance.

Through this journey, I learned that burnout is not a sign of weakness, but a warning. It is the mind's way of telling us that it cannot operate at full capacity without rest, reflection, and support.

It taught me the importance of boundaries, of listening to my body and mind, and of leaning on family and faith when the burden feels too heavy to carry alone.

Raising seven children while managing a demanding psychotherapy practice and travelling on weekends speaking at churches and events, would have been impossible without these lessons.

It required grace, intentionality, and a constant reliance on God's guidance. Matthew 11:28-30 reminded me: *"Come to me, all you who are weary and burdened, and I will give you rest. Take my yoke upon you and learn from me, for I am gentle and humble in heart, and you will find rest for your souls. For my yoke is easy and my burden is light."*

By integrating these truths into my daily life, I could continue to serve my clients, nurture my family, and maintain my own mental health.

A

hurt MIND

A hurt mind, is a real injury that affects the heart and soul, not the body. Trauma, rejection, loss, neglect, or abuse can cause these wounds. They change how we think, feel, and act. What makes them even harder to deal with is that emotional wounds often hide in places we can't see clearly.

We learn how to get by even when we're in pain. We smile even though our hearts are beating fast. We keep going, but something inside us stays stuck. I know that feeling all too well—the quiet pain that becomes a part of your daily life until you almost forget it wasn't always there.

There are many ways that a hurt mind can show up. It can look like anxiety, depression, irritability, or feeling hopeless at times. It can lead to harmful habits like eating too much, shutting down emotionally, isolating ourselves, or using drugs just to feel better for a short time. And a lot of the time, something small, like a smell, a memory, a phrase, or a situation, can bring back the pain of an old wound as if it just happened. The mind seems to go back to the moment of injury right away.

I have some wounds of my own, and for a long time I didn't even know they were there. But the body keeps track, the heart remembers, and the mind does its best to deal with things until it can't anymore. "*The Lord is close to the brokenhearted and saves those who are crushed in spirit,*" says Psalm 34:18. I used to read that verse and wonder if God could really see the bruises I was hiding. I now know that He did, and He still does.

Long-term stress and emotional pain alter the brain's circuitry. They make it harder to control your feelings, trust people, and feel safe. Isaiah 41:10 says, "*Do not be afraid, for I am with you... I will strengthen you and help you.*"

This verse can be very helpful during those times. Sometimes that help comes in the form of therapy, sometimes in the form of rest, sometimes in the form of community, and sometimes in the form of God gently putting His hand on the deepest wound in your heart.

A hurt mind can hurt the body too. Long-term stress can cause inflammation, high blood pressure, headaches, stomach problems, chest pain, a weaker immune system, and even long-term illnesses.

Our mind and body were never meant to be separate. When one is hurt, the other reacts. This is why the Bible often talks about mental and physical health together. For example, Proverbs 17:22 says, "*A cheerful heart is good medicine, but a crushed spirit dries up the bones.*"

There are many things that can hurt your mind. One of the most common causes is trauma. Trauma leaves scars that don't always go away easily, like those from abuse, neglect, violence, accidents, and disasters. Even after the danger is gone, trauma can make you feel unsafe. Being turned down can also hurt a lot.

When someone we care about pushes us away by betraying us, leaving us, fighting with us, or ignoring us, it can feel like a message that says, "You don't belong." I know how quietly it can change how you relate to people after you've felt that sting before.

Another thing that can hurt your feelings is loss. When you lose a loved one, your stability, a dream, or even yourself for a while, it can feel like there's a hole in your mind that you can't fill. There is no set time for grief; it comes and goes.

And then there is abuse, which can be physical, emotional, verbal, or sexual. Emotional abuse leaves scars that are hard to see and can last for years. It makes you doubt your value, how you see things, and who you are. "*He heals the brokenhearted and binds up their wounds*," says Psalm 147:3. It takes time to heal, but God sees the wounds we try to hide.

A hurt mind can be caused by long-term stress, like being poor, having a chronic illness, caring for others, being discriminated against, living in an unstable environment, or not getting enough emotional support. All of these things slowly wear down the mind, like water slowly cuts into stone.

A hurt mind have a lot of effects. They get in the way of trust, closeness, and connection. They can cause headaches, stomach aches, tiredness, and long-term stress. They make people anxious, depressed, have PTSD, panic attacks, and avoid things. They can make us think we don't deserve love, success, or happiness. They can make us want to be alone or numb ourselves to avoid the pain.

But healing is still possible, even with all of this. I've seen it happen to me. Over time, I've felt parts of me get softer. In memories I wanted to forget, I felt God meet me. I've seen relationships come back together, fears go away, and peace come back. Healing doesn't always go in a straight line. Some days you feel strong, and other days you feel like you can't handle it.

You might think you're better, but then something sets you off and you cry again. Just like a cut or scrape needs to be cleaned and bandaged, emotional wounds need care, understanding, and sometimes professional help.

Therapy, prayer, rest, journaling, being around other people, taking care of yourself, or even just letting yourself feel are all ways to heal. Psalm 30:2 says, "*I called to You for help, and You healed me.*" It is always possible to heal, but it doesn't always happen right away.

Every hurt mind is a story that is still being told. A lesson can be learned from every wound. There is a reason for every pain. When you don't deal with emotional wounds, they can make your mind feel chaotic and full. But when you acknowledge them and take care of them gently, your mind learns how to breathe again.

You need to get better. You deserve to be at peace. You also need to learn how to take care of your mind like you do everyone else. The next few chapters will talk about how to do that carefully and completely, one step, one breath, and one layer at a time.

A hurt mind doesn't always make noise. It often whispers. It whispers to us when we feel alone in a crowded room, when a comment hurts too much, or when a memory we thought we had forgotten comes back. I've heard this whisper many times in my own life. It's that quiet feeling that something inside me was broken, even though everyone else thought I was strong. "*The human spirit can endure a sick body, but who can bear a crushed spirit?*" (Proverbs 18:14) We forget that it's okay to say we're hurting when our outer strength hides the inner fracture.

Like ivy growing up a wall, emotional wounds can grow slowly and almost without being noticed. Trauma is often the first thing that happens. Trauma can happen in an instant, like a car accident, a violent encounter, or abuse, or it can build up over time through repeated neglect, constant criticism, or living in a home where love feels conditional.

I remember a time when I was a kid when I felt like no one was paying attention to me. It wasn't violent or extreme; it was just little, steady messages that I wasn't good enough and my feelings didn't matter.

Those messages built up over time, and I carried that weight into adulthood. That weight changed how I saw myself and others, how I dealt with stress, and how I made friends. Psalm 34:17 says, "*The righteous cry out, and the Lord hears them; he delivers them from all their troubles*." This is a comforting verse. God hears you even when you're in pain and no one else is around.

Another seed of hurt that grows quietly but deeply is rejection. It can come from friends who stop being friends, a partner who leaves, or even family members who don't show us that we are valuable.

I once got turned down in such a subtle way that I thought I was overreacting. A close friend stopped answering my calls, and I told myself that the distance was all in my head. But inside, a small crack started to form—a fear that I wasn't good enough to be with someone. The heart remembers rejection long after the mind wants to forget. Romans 8:38–39 says, "*Nothing in all of creation will be able to separate us from the love of God that is in Christ Jesus our Lord*." That love is a balm, even when people don't love you back.

The pain gets worse with loss. When we lose someone we love, whether it's through death, distance, or drifting apart, it can leave a big hole in our hearts.

I remember standing by a grave once and feeling like my chest was too heavy to carry. The sadness didn't just hurt my heart; it changed how I thought. It was hard for me to focus, sleep, or even think of happiness again.

"There is a time for everything, and a season for every activity under the heavens... a time to weep and a time to laugh, a time to mourn and a time to dance." The first step to letting myself heal was realizing that grief has its own timing.

The deepest scars are left by abuse, whether it is physical, emotional, or verbal. Emotional abuse is often hidden from the outside world, but it can be the most harmful. I know people who have had these wounds for decades because they thought they were unlovable or unworthy of care.

Gaslighting, manipulation, and constant criticism are all ways to make someone feel like they don't know what's real or how much they are worth. But healing is still possible, even in these dark places. Isaiah 61:1 says, "*The Spirit of the Sovereign Lord is on me, because the Lord has anointed me to preach good news to the poor... to bind up the brokenhearted.*" God sees the wounds that are hidden. God knows the pain that can't be seen.

Chronic stress, on the other hand, can leave scars that last a long time. Living with constant stress, money problems, or discrimination can slowly wear down the mind, making it anxious, irritable, or hopeless.

I remember a time when life felt like a never-ending list of things to do, like work, family, and other duties. There was no time to breathe. My mind was tired, my spirit was frayed, and the tension I was carrying was making my body hurt. It's not surprising that Proverbs 12:25 says, "*Anxiety weighs down the heart, but a kind word lifts it up.*" When the world feels heavy, even a little bit of support can help you start to heal.

The hurt mind also has an effect on our relationships. When we have been left, turned down, or betrayed, trust is a very fragile thing. We might be careful when making new friends or starting romantic relationships, always keeping our hearts safe. We forget how to let people in when we build walls that are too high.

I've done that—keeping people away because I thought it was too risky to let them get close. But 1 Peter 5:7 tells us to "**Cast all your anxiety on him because he cares for you.**" We can lower the walls around our wounds by letting God in, but we should do so carefully and with love.

Healing doesn't take away the pain, but it does teach us how to deal with it in ways that help us grow, connect with others, and find peace. Therapy, spiritual counselling, journaling, meditation, exercise, or just being in nature can all help you heal. It usually starts with small steps, like admitting the pain, giving it a name, and taking care of it gently.

James 5:16 says, "**So confess your sins to each other and pray for each other so that you may be healed.**" Healing is never something you do alone; it involves other people, yourself, and your spirit.

The process of healing a wounded mind is profoundly individual. There is no such thing as a perfect wound or a perfect timeline. Minor emotional wounds, such as a brief disagreement or disappointment, may heal quickly. But it can take years to get over deep wounds like trauma from childhood, abuse, or a big loss.

Some days feel like progress, while others feel like setbacks. But every time we care for ourselves, say something nice to ourselves, pray, or show ourselves compassion, we are healing.

A hurt mind does not mean you will be in prison for life. It is a story that needs to be rewritten with time, love, and faith. There is hope, even when the pain is fresh and memories come back without warning. Light exists.

God is walking next to you, ready to help you with the heavy load. Again, Psalm 147:3 says, "**He heals the brokenhearted and binds up their wounds.**" The Lord is not far away. He is there, working quietly and gently in the secret parts of our hearts.

It takes bravery to heal, but it is possible. And it starts with admitting that the pain is real, that it hurts, and that it needs to be dealt with. With prayer, support, and self-compassion, the hurt mind can slowly find peace, clarity, and even happiness again.

The next chapters will go into more detail about these paths and give people who want to come out of the shadows and into a peaceful mind practical tools, spiritual guidance, and gentle encouragement.

A
congested MIND

Sometimes I find myself wondering if anyone else's mind gets as cluttered as mine does—like there's an entire rush-hour traffic jam happening inside my head. I've had days where it felt like every thought was honking for my attention, refusing to move, refusing to let me pass.

On those days, nothing flows. My concentration slips, my memory scatters, and even the smallest decision feels like a mountain. I call it my "mentally stuck in traffic" moment. David once wrote, "*my thoughts trouble me, and I am distraught'* (Psalm 55:2), and when I read that, I felt seen. Because that's exactly how brain congestion feels—distress hidden behind a quiet face.

I've learned that this kind of mental traffic jam usually happens when I try to do too much at once or when I take in more than my heart can hold. Our world encourages nonstop movement, but our minds weren't designed to run without rest. Even Jesus stepped away from the crowds to pray and recharge (Luke 5:16). Yet sometimes I push myself past every internal boundary until my mind begs me to slow down.

There are so many reasons why our minds become "clogged," and I've personally walked through several of them.

Stress is one of the biggest culprits. I remember a season when responsibilities piled up faster than I could handle. Every morning I woke with a tight chest. Stress releases cortisol, and when cortisol stays high for too long, it clouds the mind like fog rolling over a quiet field.

Focusing becomes hard. Sleep refuses to cooperate. Everything feels heavier. *"Cast all your anxiety on Him, because He cares for you"* (1 Peter 5:7). I wish I had taken that to heart sooner instead of trying to carry everything alone.

And then there were the nights when I simply couldn't sleep. Maybe you've been there too—the kind of tired where your body wants rest, but your mind insists on staying awake. When we don't rest, the brain doesn't get to reset. Toxins build up, decision-making weakens, and suddenly even simple tasks feel overwhelming.

It's no surprise that God, in His wisdom, created night and rest as a form of healing. *"In peace I will lie down and sleep, for You alone, Lord, make me dwell in safety"* (Psalm 4:8).

I've also noticed how much my diet plays a role. During stressful seasons, I'd skip real meals and grab quick snacks, or rely on sugar and caffeine to push through. But every time, it backfired—leaving me foggy, irritable, and unfocused. Our brains, like our bodies, need nourishment.

When I began leaning into healthier habits—more fruits, more vegetables, more water—my mind slowly thanked me. Your body is a temple of the Holy Spirit (1 Corinthians 6:19), and I've realized that caring for my body is also caring for my mind.

Dehydration was something I ignored for years. There were days I'd drink everything *except* water, then wonder why my mind felt sluggish. But the brain is mostly water—so when I deprive it, it struggles to function. Headaches, fogginess, confusion… I've lived through all of them simply because I wasn't giving myself a basic necessity.

But perhaps the most profound influence on my mental clarity has always been the environment I live in and the people I'm surrounded by. When I'm around people who love me, listen to me, and give me room to be myself, my mind feels safe.

Thoughts flow freely. Emotions feel welcome. But when I've lived in spaces where I felt unheard, unseen, or emotionally neglected, my mind would close up like a clenched fist. *"A peaceful heart gives life to the body"* (Proverbs 14:30). And the opposite is just as true: an unhealthy environment steals peace from the mind.

Friendships matter too. There were seasons when I gave my trust to people who didn't handle it with care. That kind of betrayal clogs the mind with doubt, replayed moments, and lingering questions. Not everyone who smiles at us is for us—discernment is a form of protection.

Physical surroundings can exhaust the mind too. Loud noises, bright lights, chaotic spaces, cluttered rooms—they all drain mental energy. It's amazing how much clearer I think when my environment is calm and organized.

And of course, there are medical conditions that can mimic or intensify these feelings—ADHD, anxiety, depression, migraines, concussions. I've learned not to shame myself for what I can't control. God never asked me to heal myself alone. He only asked me to come to Him, all who are weary and burdened, and He promised rest (Matthew 11:28).

All these factors—stress, sleeplessness, poor diet, dehydration, toxic environments, difficult relationships, physical surroundings, and medical concerns—can pack our minds so tightly that thoughts begin running into each other. And when that happens, it's easy to feel stuck, overwhelmed, or even afraid.

But I've learned that brain congestion doesn't have to stay that way.

When I feel my mind crowding, the first thing I do is step away for a moment—just enough to breathe. I let myself pause. Sometimes I walk outside. Sometimes I sit in silence. Sometimes I talk to God and say nothing more than, "Help me calm this." And He does. ***Be still, and know that I am God*** (Psalm 46:10). Stillness doesn't fix everything instantly, but it creates room for clarity.

I've also learned to prioritize. Instead of tackling everything at once, I choose one important thing. Then another. This alone has saved me countless times from drowning in my own to-do list.

Simplifying life—physically and emotionally—brings relief too. I clean my space. I break big tasks into small steps. I release obligations God never asked me to carry. I quiet the noise of comparison, pressure, and perfectionism.

Exercise—though I used to dread it—has become a gift. Not intense workouts, just movement. A walk. Stretching. Dancing in the living room. It wakes up my mind in a way nothing else can. The joy of the Lord is your strength (Nehemiah 8:10), and sometimes joy looks like movement.

And sleep—genuine, unhurried sleep—restores me like a deep reset. A tired mind cannot think clearly, love gently, or decide wisely. Sleep is holy. It is replenishment woven into creation.

Nourishing my body helps nourish my mind. Water, good food, intentional habits—the basics matter more than I ever realized.

And then there is joy. Simple joy. Laughter. Play. Moments of delight I once dismissed. ***"A cheerful heart is good medicine"*** (Proverbs

17:22). I've found that even on heavy days, joy creates small cracks in the darkness where light can slip through.

In the end, I've learned that brain congestion is not a permanent condition—it's a signal. A warning. A gentle tap on the shoulder from the soul saying, "Please slow down. Please tend to me." And when we listen early, when we care for ourselves without guilt or shame, the mind begins to breathe again.

Like a traffic jam that eventually clears, our thoughts begin to move in rhythm once more. Our decisions become lighter. Our emotions steadier. Our hearts softer. But if we ignore the signs, the congestion can turn into combustion—a full meltdown, the kind we can no longer hide. I've reached that breaking point before, and I never want to go there again.

So now, I take my mind seriously. I treat it with tenderness. I create space for quiet, rest, nourishment, and faith. I remind myself every day that I am not alone in the journey toward clarity and peace. *"The Lord Himself goes before you and will be with you; He will never leave you nor forsake you"* (Deuteronomy 31:8).

And in that truth, my congested mind finds room to breathe again.

A
combusted MIND

There have been days when I felt like something inside me was burning, not with passion or inspiration, but with overwhelm. Combustion is usually what we use to describe fire, heat, something reacting too quickly for its own good. And for a long time, I didn't realize my mind could experience something similar.

Stressful days, pressure from every direction, the quiet weight of expectations I never asked for, and the loud noise of thoughts I didn't know how to tame — they all created a kind of internal heat that built and built until it felt like my mind was sizzling from the inside. It felt like something was burning that I couldn't put out.

I remember a season in my life when everything hit at once. Responsibilities stacked on top of each other like bricks, and every time I tried to carry them, something inside me weakened. I would lie awake at night, my heart racing even though the world was quiet. My thoughts spun like a wheel going downhill with no brakes. I didn't know back then that this was the beginning of what I now understand as mental combustion — a burnout so deep it affects the body, the emotions, and the spirit all at once.

Scripture speaks of this kind of weariness. In Psalm 61:2, it says, *"When my heart is overwhelmed, lead me to the rock that is higher than I."* At that time, I didn't know yet that I was supposed to be led, not left alone with the fire inside me.

Sometimes I think about my car when I'm trying to explain this feeling to myself. The engine is powerful, dependable, the heart of the whole vehicle. But even the strongest engine will sputter if you push it too hard for too long. It will overheat, smoke, and eventually shut down. That's exactly how my mind was functioning in those seasons — always running, never resting, always trying, never refueling.

I pushed my mental engine day after day without maintenance, without care, and without compassion. And just like a car that finally gives out on the side of the road, I found myself breaking down in moments I thought I could hold myself together. I had two cars gave up as I allowed the engine to run without oil.

God gently reminded me of the simple truth in Exodus 33:14: *"My presence will go with you, and I will give you rest."* I didn't realize that rest wasn't a luxury; it was a divine instruction.

Science tells us that our brains produce energy through a beautiful, complex process, constantly working to help us think, move, feel, and live. But even this miraculous organ has limits.

When the brain is pushed beyond what it was designed to carry, something in it starts to strain and spark. I felt it physically — the headaches, the tightness in my chest, the shortness of breath, the moments where my thoughts became so tangled that I couldn't even express what I felt.

That's what mental combustion feels like: the mind working far beyond its healthy limits until it begins to burn out. Scripture warns us about these moments more gently than any doctor could. In Proverbs 4:23, it says, *"Above all else, guard your heart, for everything you do flows from it."* I didn't realize my heart and mind were meant to be guarded, not driven like engines at full speed all the time.

The truth is, burnout doesn't happen overnight. It builds slowly, quietly, and steadily. The anxiety I brushed off, the sadness I ignored, the exhaustion I pushed through, the expectations I agreed to even when I knew I wasn't okay — all of these things created the perfect conditions for my internal fire to ignite.

A combusted mind is a kind of emotional wildfire when we don't listen to the signs our own bodies and spirits are trying to send us. Jesus once said in Matthew 11:28, *"Come to me, all who are weary and burdened, and I will give you rest."* I realize now that He was calling me long before I ever recognized the sound of His voice.

I once heard a story that felt uncomfortably familiar, because it reflected a version of me I didn't want to admit existed. It was about a woman named Gloria. She had a steady career, people who loved her, a rhythm to her days that looked good on the outside. Her life appeared perfectly put together, but inside she was crumbling. She pushed herself harder and harder, believing her value was tied to how well she performed and how little she disappointed others.

One day, she sat in an important meeting, nodding, taking notes, pretending to keep up — until suddenly she couldn't breathe. The room spun, her heart pounded, and she felt like the walls were closing in. It was her moment of combustion, her meltdown — the moment her internal fire exploded outward. She fell apart right in the middle of her success story. And as everyone rushed to her side, she realized she had ignored her needs for far too long.

Her story reminded me of myself in ways that were uncomfortable. I, too, had been the one smiling on the outside while quietly burning up on the inside.

But Gloria did something brave. She stepped back. She sought help. She let herself be supported. She simplified her life. And slowly, she healed. Her story reminded me of Psalm 147:3, where it says, *"He heals the brokenhearted and binds up their wounds."* Sometimes God binds wounds we didn't even notice we had.

A combusted mind, often shows up like a meltdown — when emotions boil over, thoughts race too fast to catch, and we no longer recognize ourselves. Stress floods the body with cortisol, and suddenly the smallest things feel impossible.

Trauma magnifies this, too. If you've been through childhood wounds, emotional neglect, or moments that left deep marks, your mind may stay on high alert even when life is peaceful. Trauma can teach the mind to burn at both ends, as though danger is always near.

Unresolved doesn't always look like a dramatic event; sometimes it looks like years of feeling unseen, unheard, or unloved. Trauma can come from childhood, relationships, loss, violence, abandonment, or even words spoken carelessly into our hearts. Trauma is like carrying shards of glass inside the mind — each sharp memory waiting to cut us whenever life bumps us too hard.

I once heard someone say that the body remembers what the mind tries to forget, and I found that painfully true. Even when I tried to move on, my mind kept replaying old wounds. Psalm 147:3 comforts me deeply: *"He heals the brokenhearted and binds up their wounds."* But healing begins only when we stop pretending the wounds aren't there.

Anxiety joins in, adding endless worry, racing thoughts, pounding heartbeats, and the feeling of never being fully safe.

Daily anxiety can also ignite the flame. Anxiety is like walking through life expecting danger at every corner. The brain stays on alert, scanning for potential threats even when there aren't any. It is exhausting — physically, mentally, spiritually.

Anxiety makes tiny problems feel like mountains and ordinary tasks feel like burdens. When anxiety grows unchecked, it irritates the mind until thoughts become tangled and frantic. Suddenly everything feels urgent. Everything feels overwhelming. Everything feels unsafe. And in that state, the mind begins to burn out.

Depression, too, adds its weight — the heaviness, the hopelessness, the loss of interest in what once brought joy. All of these create the perfect storm for mental combustion.

Depression doesn't always appear as sadness. Sometimes it's numbness. Sometimes it's silence. Sometimes it's the inability to care about the things you used to love. It's waking up already exhausted. It's smiling while something inside you feels heavy and hollow at the same time. Depression drains the mind of its energy, making even simple tasks feel monumental. This heaviness becomes more fuel for combustion. Psalm 34:18 reminds me that *"**The Lord is close to the brokenhearted and saves those who are crushed in spirit**."* Even in the darkest fog, God sits with us. But the fog itself can be suffocating.

Another cause is overstimulation — the constant noise of life. Phones buzzing, screens glowing, responsibilities stacking, global news pouring into your heart, messages demanding your attention, the endless expectation to respond instantly, produce more, achieve more, be more.

When the world doesn't stop, your mind doesn't either. And a mind that never stops eventually overheats. We weren't designed to carry the world in our pockets. We were designed to walk with God daily, not live as if we are the center of everything.

Then there are emotional burdens — unresolved guilt, unspoken fears, deep disappointments, or grief tucked away behind forced smiles. I personally learned how emotional weight collects slowly, like dust. You don't notice it day by day, but suddenly one morning you wake up feeling suffocated. That suffocation is a warning sign. A buildup. An overload. The beginning of combustion.

Loneliness adds its own spark. Not the loneliness of being physically alone, but the kind where you feel unseen even in a crowded room. This loneliness erodes the mind's resilience, making struggles feel heavier and burdens feel impossible to handle. God knew we would need connection, which is why He declared, *"It is not good for man to be alone."* Yet many of us walk through our hardest battles isolated, pretending to be fine because we fear being judged or misunderstood.

Another major cause is perfectionism. The belief that we must get everything right, be everything to everyone, and never disappoint anyone. Perfectionism is a quiet poison. It eats away at peace. It convinces us that rest is laziness, boundaries are selfish, and mistakes are unacceptable.

I lived in that mindset for a long time, and it turned my mind into a furnace — constantly burning, never resting, always demanding more from myself. God never told us to be perfect; He told us to be faithful. Matthew 11:28 gently calls, *"Come to me, all you who are weary and burdened, and I will give you rest."* Perfectionism brings burnout, but God brings rest.

Lack of self-care is one of the biggest contributors to combustion. So many of us care for others better than we care for ourselves. We pour out until we are empty, forgetting that even Jesus withdrew from the crowds to rest and pray. If the Son of God needed moments of quiet restoration, why do we think we don't?

Ignoring warning signs is what takes a simmering mind into full combustion. The headaches, irritability, emotional numbness, tearfulness, forgetfulness, restlessness, tension, and exhaustion are whispers from the mind saying, "Please slow down." When those whispers go ignored long enough, they become screams. They become meltdowns. They become breakdowns. They become combustion.

During my own difficult seasons, I found myself neglecting things I didn't think mattered — sleep, nutrition, fresh air, laughter, hydration, movement, and even prayer. And of course, neglect eventually becomes a lifestyle if we're not careful.

When we don't care for ourselves, it's not just the mind that burns — the spirit dims too. Yet scripture reminds us in 1 Kings 19 how even Elijah, a mighty prophet, burned out under pressure. He collapsed under a tree and begged God to take his life. Instead, God sent rest, food, water, and gentleness.

If one of the greatest spiritual figures in history needed rest and compassion, who am I to believe I should need less?

When combustion has gone on for too long, the mind becomes noisy — a place where thoughts bounce around without pause, where worries echo, and where focus becomes a distant dream.

I have lived through seasons where my mind felt like a radio stuck between stations, full of static, blaring everything and nothing at once. This "noisy brain" makes it hard to think clearly, pray clearly, or even feel like yourself. But God is not absent in the noise. Isaiah 26:3 says, ***"You will keep in perfect peace those whose minds are stayed on you."*** Peace is still possible, even in mental chaos.

A combusted mind can be a symptom of many things: anxiety, depression, ADHD, hormonal imbalance, exhaustion, or emotional overload. Yet even then, the tools of healing begin with awareness. It begins with recognizing the noise, the heat, the burnout — and treating yourself with compassion rather than condemnation.

With rest, nourishment, prayer, breathing, boundaries, and the courage to let go of perfection, the mind can quiet again. It can heal. It can breathe. And it can return to peace.

A combusted mind can feel powerful and frightening, but it doesn't have power over you. The mind was never created to be your master.

Scripture reminds us gently in 2 Timothy 1:7 that *"**God has not given us a spirit of fear, but of power, love, and a sound mind**."*

A sound mind is your inheritance. Peace is your promise. Rest is your right. And healing is not only possible — it is already reaching for you.

Even now, in this moment, God is not asking you to push harder. He is inviting you to breathe, to slow down, to rest, to recover, to release what burns you from the inside. He is inviting you to step out of the flames and into His arms, where your mind can finally stop fighting and start healing.

And you deserve that healing — not because you've earned it, but because He loves you. And because your mind, your heart, and your soul were never meant to burn out. They were meant to live in peace.

There are days when my mind feels like it's stuck in the middle of rush-hour traffic. Thoughts pile up behind each other, honking, pushing, refusing to wait their turn.

It feels like I'm sitting in the driver's seat of my own head with no way to steer, no open lane, and no chance to move forward. I've tried to explain this feeling to people before, but the closest comparison is mental gridlock — that overwhelming congestion inside the mind when everything arrives at once and nothing gets processed.

Scripture captures this experience in Psalm 94:19: *"**When anxiety was great within me, your consolation brought me joy**."* Even when my inner world feels like a highway jammed from end to end, God still offers comfort.

I've had moments where my mind felt so cluttered that it was like walking into a room where the floor is covered with things you meant to put away "later," but later never came. The clutter grows. The space shrinks. Even thinking becomes exhausting.

I remember one particular week when everything hit at once — deadlines, unexpected news, family responsibilities, and the pressure to be okay even when I wasn't. My mind felt swollen with thoughts I didn't have time to sort out. That was when I realized how easy it is to lose your peace without even noticing it slipping away.

Our brains are beautifully designed and incredibly capable, but even the strongest machines break down when overloaded. God created our minds with limits, not to punish us, but to remind us of the importance of balance and rest.

Ecclesiastes 3:1 says, *"To everything there is a season."* Even thinking has its season. Even silence has its purpose. But when I tried to live like every moment was a time to think, decide, respond, fix, handle, or achieve, my mind grew congested — and I didn't know how to unclog it.

There are so many things that contribute to that stuck feeling. Stress is a big one. Stress sneaks into the mind like fog rolling in slowly, and before you know it, you can't see clearly.

I used to underestimate what stress did to me. I thought if I ignored it, it would ignore me. But stress doesn't work that way. It releases chemicals into the brain that interrupt clear thinking and disrupt memory. Proverbs 12:25 says, *"Anxiety weighs down the heart."* I didn't realize how heavy my thoughts had become until I felt myself sinking under their weight.

Sleep — or the lack of it — plays a huge role too. There were nights when sleep ran away from me as though it was hiding, and I was too tired to chase it. I would lie in bed with my eyes closed but my mind wide awake, rethinking old conversations, worrying about tomorrow, replaying what went wrong yesterday.

The next day I would be tired, irritable, unfocused, and unable to string my thoughts together. It wasn't laziness. It was exhaustion. God knew we would need rest, which is why He created nighttime, and why

Psalm 127:2 reminds us that *"**He grants sleep to those He loves**."* I didn't know how loved I truly was, because I rarely allowed myself to rest.

Not everyone around us always has good intentions, and I learned that painfully. People I thought I could trust turned out to be temporary. Some friendships drained me more than they filled me.

Some atmospheres felt heavy, toxic, or unpredictable. Being surrounded by the wrong voices sharpens the noise in your mind until you can't tell which thoughts are yours and which are the echoes of negativity around you. Proverbs 13:20 warns, *"**Walk with the wise and become wise. For a companion of fools suffers harm**."* I didn't realize how many of my thoughts were shaped by environments that were slowly suffocating me.

And then there were the physical factors — things like noise, clutter, bright lights, toxins, and overstimulation. I used to brush those off, thinking I was being dramatic. But the truth is, the brain picks up more than we realize. Loudness fatigues the mind. Clutter distracts it. Toxins alter its chemistry. Everything in our environment interacts with our mental peace.

There are also deeper layers we don't always talk about — medical conditions, hormonal changes, neurological differences, concussions, migraines, chemical imbalances. These are not flaws.

They are realities. They do not define us, but they do affect how we think and feel. And sometimes, they create mental congestion that cannot be fixed with a nap or a walk or a glass of water.

Sometimes they require professional help, and seeking help is not a sign of weakness. It is a step toward healing and wisdom. Proverbs 11:14 says, *"**In the multitude of counselors there is safety**."* I had to learn that safety is not just physical protection but emotional clarity, too.

When I finally realized how congested my mind had become, the first thing I did was breathe. Not perfectly, not deeply, not even steadily

— just enough to create a moment between me and the chaos in my head. That's when I remembered God's whisper in Psalm 46:10: "*Be still, and know that I am God.*" Stillness is not inactivity. It is permission — permission to pause, to release, to reset.

The mind can heal. The heart can clear. The mental traffic can flow again. Not instantly, but gently. One breath, one prayer, one step, one small act of self-compassion at a time.

And you deserve that healing — not because you've done everything right, but because you are human, loved, and known by God. Even your cluttered thoughts are held gently in His hands.

What causes a mind to combust is rarely one single moment. It's usually a long chain of small, overlooked moments — the quiet things we ignore, the emotions we swallow, the expectations we carry, and the battles we fight in silence.

For me, it never started with an explosion. It began slowly, subtly, almost invisibly, until one day I realized that the slow burn inside me had grown into a fire I could no longer control.

There were seasons when I carried pressure like a backpack filled with bricks, but I convinced myself it was simply part of "being strong." Yet even Jesus, in His humanity, felt the weight of pressure in the garden of Gethsemane. Luke 22:44 says, "*Being in anguish, He prayed more earnestly, and His sweat was like drops of blood falling to the ground.*" If the Son of God Himself felt pressure that intense, why would I believe I must pretend to feel nothing?

A combustion mind is not a sign of weakness but a sign of being human in a world that demands too much from us. It is the result of carrying what was never meant to be carried alone. And yet, even in the collapse, there is hope. Psalm 61:2 says, "*When my heart is overwhelmed, lead me to the rock that is higher than I.*" When the mind burns out, God becomes the cool place, the safe place, the shelter.

And healing is always possible — even from combustion. Because no matter how fiercely the mind has burned, God can calm the flames, rebuild the ruins, and restore peace where chaos once lived.

A
noisy MIND

Sometimes, our minds feel like a crowded room with every radio station turned on at once. Thoughts race like cars in a traffic jam, memories pop up like unwelcome notifications, and worries swirl like autumn leaves caught in a windstorm.

A noisy mind can feel like having multiple tabs open at the same time—each one demanding your attention, making it impossible to focus on any single task. It's like hosting a rowdy party in your head while all you want is a quiet corner to think.

I remember waking up one morning before a big presentation at work, my mind buzzing like a swarm of bees. My thoughts jumped from the trivial—"Do I have everything in my bag? Did I lock the door?"— to the distracting—"What will my colleague think of my proposal? Did I text my friend back?"

Even the simplest tasks, like finding my car keys, felt like monumental hurdles. By the time I reached my desk, I was already exhausted. Instead of preparing, I scrolled through emails and social media, feeding the chaos. And when I finally stood in front of the audience, my anxiety had peaked, my focus scattered, and I felt I had delivered anything but my best.

This is the noisy brain in action. It's like a messy room: items everywhere, impossible to navigate. Or a TV that never turns off, even when no one is watching. It's a brain full of distractions, racing thoughts, and random memories—some embarrassing, some stressful—that make it nearly impossible to concentrate.

The Bible reminds us that even Jesus experienced mental and emotional burden: *"Come to me, all you who are weary and burdened, and I will give you rest"* (Matthew 11:28). This is not just spiritual comfort—it's practical wisdom. Quieting the mind requires intention, effort, and the gentle patience that comes from trusting God's guidance.

I've found that a noisy brain often has deeper roots. Stress, lack of sleep, or hormonal changes can trigger it. Disorders like ADHD, traumatic brain injuries, or neurological conditions can amplify the chatter. Even environmental factors—bright lights, loud sounds, constant stimulation—can make it worse.

But beyond the physical, there's the emotional: wounds from past hurts, unresolved trauma, or ongoing anxiety can create a state of hyperarousal in the mind, keeping it in a constant fight-or-flight mode.

You can focus, be present, and find moments of stillness even in a busy world. And as Philippians 4:6-7 encourages us: *"Do not be anxious about anything, but in every situation, by prayer and petition, with thanksgiving, present your requests to God. And the peace of God, which transcends all understanding, will guard your hearts and your minds in Christ Jesus."*

Quieting the mind is not about eliminating thoughts; it's about creating space for clarity, focus, and peace. And when you nurture both your mind and your heart, burnout loses its grip. The noisy brain doesn't have to control you—you can manage your mind, step by step, prayer by prayer, breath by breath.

There was a week when I was juggling multiple deadlines at work while caring for a sick family member, my mother had a triple bypass. Each morning, I woke up with a knot in my stomach.

My brain seemed to have a mind of its own, replaying every possible "what if" scenario: *"What if I miss this deadline? What if something happens to my mom? Did I forget to schedule the meeting?"*

During this time, sleep was scarce, and my thoughts were relentless. I found myself in the kitchen at 2 a.m., unable to stop planning, analyzing, and worrying.

It was during one of those sleepless nights that I turned to Philippians 4:6-7: ***"Do not be anxious about anything, but in every situation, by prayer and petition, with thanksgiving, present your requests to God. And the peace of God, which transcends all understanding, will guard your hearts and your minds in Christ Jesus."***

I prayed, not asking for my mind to be quiet immediately, but for help in carrying the weight I had been shouldering alone. Gradually, I noticed a small shift. I could lie down and breathe deeply, trusting that God was in control, even if my brain refused to settle.

My "to-do" list seemed endless, and my thoughts were bouncing like ping-pong balls. I started doubting myself, fearing I wasn't capable of managing it all.

One morning, in desperation, I opened my Bible to Isaiah 41:10: ***"So do not fear, for I am with you; do not be dismayed, for I am your God. I will strengthen you and help you; I will uphold you with my righteous right hand."***

Reading those words felt like someone placed a gentle hand on my shoulder. I realized that even if my mind was noisy, God was still present, guiding me, and giving me the strength I needed.

A noisy brain is often a messenger of deeper emotional needs. Emotional wounds—unresolved grief, betrayal, or childhood trauma—can keep the mind in constant overdrive. I learned this when a childhood memory surfaced unexpectedly during a stressful season.

Quieting the mind is not about eliminating thoughts; it's about creating space for clarity, focus, and peace. Nurture both mind and heart, and burnout loses its grip.

I've felt this personally. Memories of past failures or embarrassing moments would replay endlessly in my head, like a broken record.

At night, instead of rest, my mind cataloged tasks for tomorrow, rehashed yesterday, and even fretted over things that might never happen. I wanted to scream at my brain: "Can't you just give me five minutes of peace?" But slowly, I learned to respond differently.

Psalm 46:10 says, *"Be still, and know that I am God."* This verse became my anchor. It reminded me that I don't have to control every thought or anticipate every outcome. Quiet doesn't mean empty—it means intentional. I started with small steps:

- **Mindfulness and deep breathing:** Even five minutes a day of focused breathing brought clarity.
- **Journaling:** Writing thoughts down helped me see patterns and release mental clutter.
- **Prayer and reflection:** Sharing my worries with God gave me perspective and relief.
- **Setting boundaries:** I reduced constant notifications and carved out time for rest.

Over time, these practices reshaped my mind. I could approach work tasks without feeling scattered, attend conversations without mentally wandering, and even sleep more peacefully. The noisy brain didn't vanish overnight, but each small effort made a difference.

The noisy brain also reminds us to care for the heart, because unresolved emotional wounds can drive our minds into chaos. Trauma, grief, or emotional pain may keep our brains in overdrive long after the immediate danger has passed.

Healing these wounds—through prayer, therapy, or supportive community—is essential. Isaiah 61:1 reminds us: *"**He has sent me to bind up the brokenhearted, to proclaim freedom for the captives.**"* God offers healing for the heart, which in turn quiets the mind.

Dealing with a noisy brain is a journey, not a quick fix. It requires patience, self-compassion, and intentional action. Sometimes, it's about taking a bubble bath, going for a walk, or curling up with a good book.

Other times, it's about facing our emotional wounds, seeking therapy, or leaning on God's guidance. Each step, however small, brings us closer to peace.

Remember this: a noisy brain does not define you. It is a signal—a sign that rest, reflection, and healing are needed. With time, practice, and faith, you can calm the chaos.

A

resilience MIND

I used to think resilience was something tough people were born with, a kind of spiritual callous that grew from enduring pain without flinching. Then I broke. Completely.

This chapter is the map I wish someone had handed me on the day I collapsed. Everything in it I have lived, stumbled through, and proved true on the other side. My prayer is that you will not have to hit the wall the way I did before you begin building a resilient life.

For years I treated my body like an unreliable employee who worked for my calendar. I filled every square with colour-coded appointments and congratulated myself for being a good steward of time. I was wrong.

Time is infinite; energy is not. You can always make more money, but you cannot make more energy. The Bible never commands us to redeem the time at the expense of our health; it commands us to redeem the time because the days are evil (Ephesians 5:16), and evil days require people who are alive, not zombies in Christian clothing.

When I finally admitted I was bankrupt of energy, I started a ruthless experiment. I tracked where my energy went the same way I once tracked minutes. I discovered four categories:

Green activities gave energy (worship, deep sleep, laughter with my wife, playing and being present with my children, walking in the woods while praying).

Yellow activities were neutral (most meetings, admin work, grocery shopping).

Red activities drained energy fast (scrolling social media at night, saying yes when my spirit said no, perfectionism, people-pleasing).

Black activities were soul-killers (gossip, comparison, ministry out of insecurity).

I began protecting green like it was gold and eliminating black like it was poison. I started saying a sentence I had never allowed myself to say before: "I don't have the energy for that right now, and that's okay." The first time I said it to a church member who wanted an extra meeting, I waited for lightning. Instead, grace fell. The world kept spinning.

Jesus modeled this perfectly. He poured out healing all day, then withdrew to lonely places to pray (Luke 5:16). He fed five thousand, then immediately made the disciples get into the boat so He could go recharge alone (Mark 6:45-46). He never apologized for protecting His energy. He knew the Father had an unlimited supply of power, but the Son, in His humanity, had a limited body that needed sleep, food, and solitude.

Paul understood this too: "*I discipline my body and keep it under control, lest after preaching to others I myself should be disqualified*" (1 Corinthians 9:27 ESV). He was not talking about six-pack abs; he was talking about stewarding the temple so the gospel could keep flowing through it for decades, not just a dramatic decade.

Today I manage energy first and time second. My calendar now has white space the way a healthy artery has room for blood to flow. I schedule green before I schedule yellow. I protect sleep the way Nehemiah protected the walls of Jerusalem. And I have more fruit in my forties than I ever had in my thirties when I was "busier."

Burnout is what happens when we spend our lives on something smaller than the purpose God wrote on our hearts. I know, because for years I pastored and ran a Bible College, even committed to the mission field in Croatian 1994-1997 during the war with my wife Kathleen and 3 children under the age of three, out of a need to prove I was valuable instead of out of the overflow of knowing I already was.

When my purpose was "Don't let anyone down," I burned out. When my purpose became "Love Jesus, love my family, love the people He puts in front of me today," resilience showed up like an old friend.

Purpose is the root system that keeps a tree standing in a storm. *"For I know the plans I have for you," declares the Lord, "plans to prosper you and not to harm you, plans to give you hope and a future"* (Jeremiah 29:11). When we know whose we are and why we are here, hard seasons become chapters instead of the whole book.

In the darkest stretch of recovery I sat on my back yard every morning with coffee and a blank journal. I wrote one question at the top of the page: "Lord, what is the one thing You want from my life that only I can give?" Some days the answer was "Be My son." Other days it was "Raise those children to love Me." Sometimes it was simply "Heal, so you can help others heal." But slowly a sentence formed that still anchors me: "I am here to know Jesus and make Him known with a joyful heart and a rested body."

That single sentence has saved me from a thousand detours. When an opportunity arises, I hold it up to the sentence. If it threatens the joyful heart or the rested body, the answer is no, and I don't feel guilty. Purpose clarifies everything.

Moses tried to carry Israel by himself and almost lost his mind (Exodus 18). Jethro's advice was essentially, "Son, you are not that important, and that is good news." When Moses delegated, the people were served better and Moses lasted forty more years. Purpose kept him alive.

Find your sentence. Write it in the front of your Bible. Say it out loud when the world tries to pull you off course. It will become the root system that keeps you standing when the wind howls.

Resilience is built in the quiet, daily choices no one applauds.

I started with sleep because I was desperate. For six months I treated 10:30 p.m. to 6:30 a.m. like a tithe I could not rob. *"In peace I will lie down and sleep, for you alone, Lord, make me dwell in safety"* (Psalm 4:8). I read that verse every night like a lullaby. My body began to trust that the world would not end if I closed my eyes.

Then I added movement. Nothing heroic, just thirty minutes of walking while I prayed in tongues or listened to Psalms on audio. My body had stored years of stress in my shoulders and hips; movement began to release it. *"A heart at peace gives life to the body"* (Proverbs 14:30). Science calls it somatic healing; David called it dancing before the Lord.

Food came next. I stopped treating my body like a dumpster for hurry. I started eating what actually nourished the temple (1 Corinthians 6:19-20). Sugar crashes and sermon prep stopped being roommates.

The habit that surprised me most was laughter. I had become so serious about the kingdom that I forgot joy is a fruit of the Spirit, not a distraction from it. My wife and I instituted "no-phones comedy night" once a week. We watch old sitcoms like Friends and Golden Girls and laugh until we cry. Nehemiah said the joy of the Lord is our strength (Nehemiah 8:10), and I finally believe him with my whole body.

I also started micro-Sabbaths, five-minute pauses throughout the day where I do absolutely nothing but breathe and thank God for three specific things. Science calls it vagus-nerve regulation; Jesus called it *"abide in Me"* (John 15:4).

These habits are not impressive. They are obedient. And obedience in the small things builds a resilience that shame and striving never could.

The most important discovery of my recovery was this: my brain is not fixed; it is plastic, moldable by the renewing of my mind (Romans 12:2). Neuroscientists call it neuroplasticity; Paul called it transformation.

I spent a year rewiring three specific pathways.

First, I replaced scarcity with abundance. My default setting had been "There is never enough, time, energy, money, approval." I began a daily practice of speaking abundance out loud: *"The Lord is my shepherd; I shall not want"* (Psalm 23:1). I thanked Him for every green light, every parking space, every unexpected refund. My brain began to notice evidence of provision instead of lack.

Second, I retrained my identity. Burnout had convinced me I was what I produced. I started a habit I still keep: every morning I stand in front of the mirror and say, "I am a beloved son of God, with whom He is well pleased, before I do a single thing today" (Matthew 3:17, personalized). It felt fake for weeks. Then one day it landed in my bones, and the need to perform lost its claws.

Third, I practiced pre-deciding instead of white-knuckling. I wrote down my non-negotiables when I was calm (bedtime, rest days, exercise, date night) and posted them where I could see them. When temptation came to overwork, the decision was already made. Daniel *"resolved not to defile himself"* before the king's food ever showed up (Daniel 1:8). Pre-deciding is spiritual resilience in advance.

I also started a gratitude rampage every night. Three things I'm thankful for, spoken out loud. Neuro-science says gratitude literally thickens the pre-frontal cortex and shrinks the amygdala. Scripture says it is God's will for me in Christ Jesus (1 Thessalonians 5:18). Both are right.

Nine months into these practices Kathleen said, "Your brain scans like a different person." I laughed and told her Jesus had been saying the same thing for two thousand years: *"Be transformed by the renewing of your mind."*

Today I am the most resilient I have ever been, not because life got easier, but because my roots go deeper. Storms still come. Deadlines still loom. People still disappoint. But I bounce forward instead of breaking because I have learned to manage energy, anchor in purpose, nourish body and soul with holy habits, and let the Word of God rewire my brain for balance.

And here is the best part: the same Spirit who raised Jesus from the dead is raising you right now (Romans 8:11). He is not in a hurry. He is not disappointed in your limits. He designed them so you would need Him every day, and needing Him every day is the most resilient place a human being can live.

So start tonight. Turn off the phone. Speak one truth out loud. Go to bed on time. Thank Him for three things. Repeat tomorrow.

Resilience is not a gift for the chosen few. It is a garden for anyone willing to tend it one obedient day at a time.

I am living proof. And soon, by God's stubborn grace, you will be too.

CONCLUSION

You have just closed the final page of a journey that very few people ever finish.

Most never even begin. They live their entire lives with a mind that feels like a battlefield, a junkyard, or a burning building, and they call it "normal." They numb it with scrolling, shopping, alcohol, achievement, or endless noise. They assume the racing thoughts, the dread in the chest, the sudden tears, the rage that comes out of nowhere, the fog that makes even simple decisions feel impossible, are just the price of being alive in this century.

But you refused to settle for that lie. You picked up this book, you turned every page, you did the exercises, you wept in some chapters, you shouted "yes" in others, and somewhere along the way something irreversible happened: you woke up.

You woke up to the truth that your mind is not your enemy. It is not a broken machine. It is not doomed to chaos. It is a masterpiece designed by a Master Craftsman, fearfully and wonderfully made, endowed with a plasticity that can rewrite decades of damage, endowed with a Spirit who is willing and able to renew it day by day.

You woke up to the realization that the chaos you have lived with was never the plan. Peace is your birthright. Clarity is your inheritance. Dominion over your thought life is not a nice bonus for super-spiritual people; it is the baseline from which every son and daughter of God is meant to operate.

Let's take one long, slow walk together through everything that has happened inside you while you read these pages, so that nothing is lost, so that every truth is sealed into your bones.

You began by facing the uncomfortable but liberating reality of an affected mind. You looked squarely at the voices that were planted in childhood, the labels that stuck, the traumas that rewired your nervous system, the cultural scripts you absorbed without consent.

You saw how comparison, rejection, shame, and performance became the operating system you never chose. And instead of shaming yourself for being affected, you heard Jesus whisper, "You are not dirty because you were hurt. You are beloved, and I am not afraid of your history." That was the first crack of light.

From there you learned to recognize a burnout mind long before it collapses. You now know the seven hidden stages, how emotional exhaustion sneaks in wearing the mask of "I'm fine," how depersonalization turns people into tasks and tasks into burdens, how reduced accomplishment convinces you that you are failing when you are actually depleted.

You know the physiological truth that chronic cortisol literally shrinks your prefrontal cortex and enlarges your amygdala, turning you into a more primitive version of yourself. But more importantly, you now carry the early-warning system God placed in your body: the tightness in your chest, the dread on Sunday night, the rage over tiny things, the tears that come for no apparent reason. These are not weaknesses; they are smoke alarms. And you have learned never to unplug a smoke alarm again.

You sat with the tender places next. A hurt mind. You finally gave yourself permission to call betrayal betrayal, abuse abuse, abandonment abandonment. You stopped spiritualizing pain away with premature "I forgive" statements that left the arrows still lodged in your soul.

You learned that trauma is not a faith failure; it is a neurological injury, and that Jesus is the Gentle Surgeon who knows exactly where every shard of glass is buried. You discovered that forgiveness and healing are not the same thing, that you can release a person and still need to heal the damage they left behind.

You cried when you read Psalm 147:3 and realized for the first time that binding up wounds is something God still does today, in therapy offices, in prayer rooms, in the middle of the night when you finally tell Him the whole ugly story and He does not flinch.

Then came the chapters that felt like unclogging a drain that had been backed up for years. A congested mind. A noisy mind. A combusted mind. You saw how 100,000 words a day, 3,000 advertising messages, endless notifications, and the 24-hour trauma cycle of the internet had turned your beautiful brain into a hoarder house of junk data.

You learned why panic attacks feel like dying, because to your primitive brain they are dying, threat detection gone haywire. But you also learned the first-aid kit: 4-7-8 breathing, grounding techniques, the power of naming what is happening ("This is a wave, not a tsunami; it will pass"), and the ultimate weapon, declaring Scripture out loud until the adrenaline subsides and the voice of Truth is louder than the voice of terror.

And then, sweet relief, brain dumping. Ten minutes that changed everything. You discovered that getting the swarm out of your head and onto paper is not a productivity hack; it is spiritual warfare.

You saw David doing it in the cave of Adullam, Habakkuk doing it on the watchtower, Paul doing it from a Roman prison. You learned that the simple act of writing "I feel…" or "I'm afraid that…" or "Lord, here is everything" is often the moment the dam breaks and peace floods back in. You now have a lifelong habit that costs nothing and returns everything.

From dumping you moved to weeding. You finally looked at the recurring thoughts that had been choking the life out of you: bitterness that felt justified, envy that felt spiritual, perfectionism that felt like excellence, shame that felt like humility.

You learned the difference between conviction and condemnation, between repentance and self-hatred. You practiced the Philippians 4:8 audit: Is this thought true? Noble? Right? Pure? Lovely? Admirable? Excellent? Praiseworthy? And when the answer was no, you uprooted it, not by willpower but by replacement, planting Scripture where the weed had been. You discovered that "taking every thought captive" is not a Marine-Corps slogan; it is gardening with the Holy Spirit.

With the weeds gone, decluttering felt possible. You cleaned your physical spaces and realized the direct neurological link between a chaotic environment and a chaotic mind. You deleted apps, unsubscribed, turned off notifications, said no to good things so you could say yes to God things.

You learned that minimalism is not a trend; it is obedience to *"Let all things be done decently and in order"* (1 Corinthians 14:40). You gave your brain literal room to breathe.

You stepped beyond burnout into a life that no longer flirts with collapse. You rediscovered Sabbath not as a day off but as a weekly non-negotiable act of trust. You learned to set boundaries without guilt, to rest without laziness, to receive limits as gifts from a kind Father who knows you are dust. You began to practice delight again, play, beauty, laughter, hobbies that have no productive outcome, because joy is not a luxury; it is brain medicine.

Then came the rebuilding. Brain reconditioning, restructuring, regrouping. You saw the science of neuroplasticity confirm the promise of Romans 12:2. You began meditating on Scripture not as a duty but as a rewiring session, repeating truth until neural pathways literally thickened in the areas of peace, gratitude, and self-control.

You practiced gratitude until it changed the chemical balance of your brain. You fasted and felt the fog lift. You confessed sin and watched strongholds crumble. You learned that repentance is not groveling; it is renovation.

You started brain training like an athlete. Five minutes of breath prayer. Ten minutes of silence. Memory verses that became mental armor. You discovered that the same discipline that builds biceps builds focus, that the spiritual disciplines are simultaneously neurological disciplines. You stopped seeing training as optional and started seeing it as survival.

You became ruthless about brain feeding. You curated your inputs the way a diabetic curates sugar. You asked of every podcast, every feed, every conversation: Does this nourish or deplete? Does this feed faith or fear? You learned that "guard your heart" begins with guard your eyes and ears. You began to starve anxiety and feast on truth, beauty, and goodness until your default emotional state began to shift.

You built a brain maintenance plan that will outlast this book: sleep, movement, hydration, community, therapy when needed, daily encounter with Jesus. You stopped treating self-care as selfish and started treating it as stewardship of the temple God lives in.

You built resilience, not by becoming tougher but by becoming more anchored in Christ. You learned that resilience is elasticity, the ability to bend without breaking, to absorb shock and spring back.

You practiced the spiritual muscle of "in everything give thanks," of preaching to yourself instead of listening to yourself, of choosing to rejoice until the feeling catches up.

You discovered the staggering privilege of thinking tandem with the Holy Spirit. You began to notice the gentle checks, the sudden Scriptures that drop into your mind, the peace that acts like a referee. You realized that "we have the mind of Christ" is not hyperbole; it is an operating system upgrade available right now.

And finally, you stepped into brain renewal and brain mastering. You now live, most days, from a place of dominion instead of defense. You catch thoughts before they catch you. You renew your mind not once but hourly.

You walk in peace that actually does surpass understanding because it does not depend on circumstances. You have learned to master impulsivity, to master fear, to master the tongue that is set on fire by hell by setting it on fire with heaven first.

You are not the same person who began this book.

You used to think peace was the absence of problems. Now you know peace is the presence of Jesus in the middle of problems.

You used to think strength was never feeling weak. Now you know strength is running to the One who is strong when you have none left.

You used to think renewal was a one-time event. Now you know it is a lifestyle of returning, again and again, to the One who makes all things new.

You used to think mastering your mind was about perfect performance. Now you know it is about perfect surrender, moment by moment, thought by thought, breath by breath.

You have learned that the battlefield is the mind, and the victory is already won. The enemy's only remaining weapon is deception, and you have put on the helmet of salvation, the belt of truth, the breastplate of righteousness.

You wield the sword of the Spirit, which is the spoken Word of God. You stand behind the shield of faith, behind which every fiery dart is extinguished.

You have learned that burnout is not inevitable. It is not the price of loving people or working hard or living in a broken world. Burnout is what happens when we try to live the supernatural Christian life with natural strength alone. But you no longer live with natural strength alone. You live plugged into the inexhaustible power source of the risen Christ.

You have learned that the same Spirit who raised Jesus from the dead lives in you and is willing to quicken your mortal body, your mortal emotions, your mortal mind. You have learned to say, with growing confidence, *"The Lord is my shepherd, I lack nothing. He makes me lie down in green pastures, he leads me beside quiet waters, he refreshes my soul."*

You have learned to pray dangerous prayers: *"Search me, God, and know my heart; test me and know my anxious thoughts. See if there is any offensive way in me, and lead me in the way everlasting."* And you have discovered that He is gentle with the tender places and fierce with the strongholds.

You have learned that community is not optional. That bearing one another's burdens is not a suggestion. That there is no shame in therapy, in medication when needed, in saying "I need help." You have surrounded yourself with people who point you back to Jesus when your thoughts lie, who remind you who you are when you forget.

You have learned to preach the gospel to yourself every day, because you forget every day. You remind yourself that you are forgiven, accepted, beloved, empowered, sealed, kept. You remind yourself that nothing can separate you from the love of God, neither height nor depth nor racing thoughts nor panic attacks nor burnout nor trauma nor anything else in all creation.

You have learned to end each day with a brain dump of gratitude, to fall asleep rehearsing the faithfulness of God instead of rehearsing the failures of the day.

You have learned that the goal is not a perfect mind but a surrendered mind, not a life without storms but a life with an anchor.

And now, as you close this book, you carry something no one can take from you: the lived experience that Jesus is real in the places no one sees, that renewal is possible on a Tuesday afternoon when the kids are screaming and the inbox is exploding, that peace is not the absence of trouble but the presence of a Person.

You are not finished. You will never be finished this side of heaven. There will be new battles, new weeds, new congestion, new temptations to hustle for worthiness. But you will never again fight unarmed. You know where to run. You know who to call. You know whose you are.

So go.

Live the renewed mind.

Love with the renewed heart.

Work with the renewed strength.

Rest with the renewed trust.

The world is desperate for people whose minds are stayed on Christ, whose peace is palpable, whose joy is contagious, whose resilience is supernatural. The world is desperate for you.

Master your mind, not so you can lord it over others, but so you can love them better.

Master your mind, not so you can escape pain, but so you can carry it without being crushed.

Master your mind, not so you can perform for God, but so you can enjoy Him forever.

The fire is out.

The garden is growing.

The Master is smiling.

And you, beloved, are just getting started.

www.ingramcontent.com/pod-product-compliance
Lightning Source LLC
Chambersburg PA
CBHW071736120626
46550CB00002B/538